OTHER PRODUCTIVITY BOOKS BY V. DANIEL HUNT

Reengineering—Leveraging the Power of Integrated Product Development. Essex Junction, Vermont: Oliver Wight/Omneo, 1993.

Quality Management for Government: A Guide to Federal, State and Local Implementation. Milwaukee, WI: American Society of Quality Control. Quality Press, 1993.

Quality in America—How to Implement a Competitive Quality Program. Burr Ridge, IL: Irwin Professional Publishing, 1992.

Managing Quality. Homewood, IL: Business One Irwin, 1992.

Enterprise Integration Sourcebook. San Diego, CA: Academic Press, 1991.

Understanding Robotics. San Diego, CA: Academic Press, 1990.

Computer-Integrated Manufacturing Handbook. New York: Routledge, Chapman & Hall, 1989.

Superconductivity Sourcebook. New York: John Wiley and Sons, 1989.

Robotics Sourcebook. New York: Elsevier Science Publishing Company, 1988.

Dictionary of Advanced Manufacturing Technology. New York: Elsevier Science Publishing Company, 1987.

Mechatronics: Japan's Newest Threat. New York: Chapman & Hall, 1987.

Artificial Intelligence and Expert System Sourcebook. New York: Chapman & Hall, 1986.

Smart Robots. New York: Chapman & Hall, 1985.

THE SURVIVAL FACTOR

An Action Guide to Improving Your Business Today

V. DANIEL HUNT

omneo

AN IMPRINT OF OLIVER WIGHT PUBLICATIONS, INC.
85 Allen Martin Drive
Essex Junction, Vermont 05452

Published by Oliver Wight Publications, Inc.

Oliver Wight Publications books may be purchased for educational,
business, or sales promotional use. For information, please call
or write: Special Sales Department, Oliver Wight Publications,
Inc., 85 Allen Martin Drive, Essex Junction, VT 05452.
Telephone: (800) 343-0625 or (802) 878-8161; FAX: (802) 878-3384.

Library of Congress Catalog Card Number: 93-076395

ISBN: 0-939246-65-1

Text design by Irving Perkins Associates

Printed on acid-free paper.

Manufactured in the United States of America.

1   2   3   4   5   6   7   8   9   10

To Janet Claire Hunt
The Love of My Life

Contents

Illustrations

Tables

Acknowledgments

The Survival Factor has been developed based on information from a wide variety of authorities who are specialists in their respective fields. The following publications were used as intellectual resources for this book:

Quality in America—How to Implement a Competitive Quality Program. V. Daniel Hunt. Irwin Professional Publishing, Burr Ridge, IL: 1992.

Reengineering—Leveraging the Power of Integrated Product Development. V. Daniel Hunt. Oliver Wight/Omneo, Essex Junction, VT: 1993.

The continuous process improvement steps in this book are based on *An Introduction to the Continuous Improvement Process— Principles and Practices,* by Nicholas R. Schacht and Brian E. Mansir, April 1989, developed by LMI under DoD contract MDA903-85-C-0139. We thank DoD and LMI for permission to use this material. This material has been revised to emphasis the role of continuous process improvement in business survival situations.

This manuscript was word processed by Mrs. Valerie J. Western. The internal graphic design was provided by Mr. Karl J. Samuels.

Many individuals provided materials, interview comments, and their insights regarding how to improve your business, and help assure your business survival, by adopting near-term practical improvements for your business processes. I appreciate their input and help in defining this book.

The author thanks Kenan S. Abosch for providing information on broad banding. The material in chapter 11 is an abridgment of Hewitt Associates LLC material on broad banding. Hewitt Associates LLC is the leading authority on broad banding. For more information contact Mr. Abosch at Hewitt Associates, 100 Half Day Road, Lincolnshire, IL: 60069, (708) 295-5000.

The Handbook for Decline is an abridged version of material (pages 270–272) from *Profits in the Dark—How Xerox Reinvented Itself and Beat Back the Japanese*, by David T. Kearns and David A. Nadler, published by HarperBusiness, New York, 1992. Reprinted by permission of HarperBusiness.

We thank the following authors and publishers for permission to quote from their books.

Post-Capitalist Society, Peter F. Drucker, New York, HarperBusiness, 1993.

The West Point Way of Leadership, Larry R. Donnithorne, Currency Doubleday, 1993.

Total Quality Control for Management: Strategies and Tactics from Toyota and Toyota Gosei, ed. and trans. David Lu. Englewood Cliffs, NJ: Prentice Hall, 1987.

Control Your Destiny or Someone Else Will, by Noel M. Tichy and Stratford Sherman, Currency Doubleday, 1993.

Reengineering The Corporation, Michael Hammer and James Champy, HarperCollins Publishers Inc., New York, 1993.

Competitive Benchmarking: What It Is and What It Can Do For You, prepared by Xerox Corporate Quality Office, Stamford, Connecticut, 1987.

Competitive Benchmarking: The Path to a Leadership Position, prepared by Xerox Corporate Quality Office, Stamford, Connecticut, 1988.

Leadership Through Quality Training Programs: A Guide to Benchmarking in Xerox. It is available through a partnership with the U.S. Department of Commerce, National Technical Information Services (NTIS), in Springfield Va. The NTIS document number is PB91-780106.

Dynamic Manufacturing—Creating the Learning Organization, by

Robert H. Hayes, Steven C. Wheelwright, and Kim B. Clark, The Free Press, 1988.

A Guide for Implementing Total Quality Management, Reliability Analysis Center state-of-the-art report, Report SOAR-7, Rome NY, Rome AFB, 1990.

Portions of Cover Story entitled *"The Pain of Downsizing,"* from the May 9, 1994 issue of *Business Week* has been reproduced with the permission of McGraw-Hill.

Pay for Performance—What You Should Know by Linda Thornburg, June 1992, reprinted with the permission of HRMagazine published by the Society for Human Resources Management, Alexandria, VA.

How Do You Cut the Cake?, by Linda Thornburg, October 1992, reprinted with the permission of HRMagazine, published by the Society for Human Resource Management, Alexandria, VA.

Pay That Rewards Knowledge, by Thomas J. Krajci, June 1990, reprinted with the permission of HRMagazine, published by the Society for Human Resource Management, Alexandria, VA.

"Who Needs a Boss", by Brian Dumaine, Fortune Magazine, May 7, 1990.

Table 7.2 "The Traumatic Impact of Downsizing" is adapted with permission from the *Journal of Psychosomatic Research*, vol. II. "The Social Readjustment Scale," T. H. Holmes and R. H. Rahe. Pergamon Press, 1967.

Leadership Transition, Team Building, Team Effectiveness Assessments; and New Team Start-up, Organizational Assessment—An Overview for Managers, U.S. Government, USDA-APHIS-HRD, prepared by Dan Stone, Hyattsville, MD. 20782.

Functional Process Simulation Guidebook, U.S. Government, Director of Defense Information, 1 January 1993, Washington D.C. 20301.

Increasing Organizational Return, Sibson & Company, Inc., 1993, reproduced with the Permission of Sibson & Company. Figure on page 4 entitled "Most Companies Agree that Certain Conditions are Critical to Success."

THE
SURVIVAL
FACTOR

CHAPTER 1

To Survive-Act Now!

It seems that every business leader has the same initial question: "What can you do for me today?" For all the talk about new management initiatives, such as reengineering, downsizing, work-flow analysis, process mapping, policy deployment, teamwork, and performance pay incentives, business leaders are still looking for the "quick fix." They often do not recognize the most effective ways to survive pressing competitive pressures—by taking near-term proven action steps to turn their business around.

Every business is under pressure to change. For many businesses, earnings are declining, and operating and labor costs as a percentage of sales are still increasing. Many business leaders such as you believe that it takes too long to get things done—to reduce the costs of production and service operations, to improve quality to assure customer satisfaction, and to bring new products and services to your customers faster, in order to satisfy their needs.

This chapter sets the stage for you to increase your chance of survival by beginning now to improve your performance by focusing on the key survival factors presented in this book.

TEN STEPS TO BUSINESS FAILURE

It is important in your search for near-term action steps to know what you shouldn't do, as well as what you should—as illustrated by the positive action steps described in the balance of this book. David Kearns, former CEO of Xerox, in his book *Profits in the Dark*,[1] created what he called a handbook for competitive decline, a succinct set of instructions that many business leaders currently are following that will put your company out of business. If you already are following these steps to business failure, don't expect to be around much longer. The Kearns course of action has been abridged and adapted for the survival factors, and each of these wrong ways to do business is described below.

Step 1: Assume You Know Your Customer

This first step instructs you to assume you know the customer, that you know what he wants better than he does, and that he will remain loyal to you no matter how much you abuse him. This step also advises you not to waste time measuring customer satisfaction and definitely not to pay attention to or respond to customer complaints. Who does that customer think he is anyway!

Step 2: Don't Invest in Quality

This follows nicely from the first step. It assumes that the customer doesn't care one bit about quality and won't notice any differences in quality between one product and another. So don't even try to meet customer requirements. Do whatever you want. Don't bother to improve work processes and reduce rework errors.

Step 3: Ignore Product Design

This argues that you don't have to fret about product design and the aesthetics of your products and services. After all, design costs money. Why should customers care what anything looks like?

Step 4: Deemphasize Manufacturing

Don't pay too much attention to how the product is made, to understanding and improving your manufacturing process, or to the relationship among design, development, engineering, and production. Keep anyone with manufacturing experience well away from the executive suite. The true secret of success is to completely get out of the business of producing things yourself.

Step 5: Avoid the Low End Products or Services

Listen, there's not much money to be made there, the margins are ludicrous, you have to spend so much time on process improvements just to save a few pennies, and the competition is brutal. Foreign competitors who jump into the low end don't have the capacity or skill to move into the bigger markets, so why worry?

Step 6: Do It Alone

We all know that real men (or women) don't eat quiche, and real men don't do joint ventures. So if you're a real man, and any good at what you do, steer clear of entangling alliances, partnerships, and confusing joint arrangements. Do it all yourself.

Step 7: Underestimate Your Competition

Don't lose any sleep over your competitors. They're probably not any good, anyway. Relax and assume that the competition is standing still and you can plan to compete tomorrow with what they have in the market today. Be comforted by the fact that your competitors have always depended more on luck than expertise, and no one stays lucky forever.

Step 8: Organize Traditionally

Nothing beats traditional organizational structures and processes—especially when they include disorganized and duplicated work, multiple organizational hierarchies, and large, powerful nonproductive corporate staffs. Cut your costs by firing people, but make sure you maintain the same basic approaches to organizing your business. It got you this far!

Step 9: Develop Talent Narrowly

Keep your people, especially management, focused closely on their own special business function, speciality, product, or niche. Why worry about the broad development of people over time? They won't be around later anyway.

Step 10: Don't Question Success

Assume that the sources of your success in the past will continue to be the seeds of triumph in the future. Don't dwell on failures or reflect on mistakes. There are no lessons there. If it worked before, it will work again. If it ain't broke, don't even think about fixing it.

This list seems ridiculous. But take a look at your own style of management. How many of the ten steps to business failure are you practicing currently?

As David Kearns stated in his book, it's fair to say Xerox did just fine by applying nine of the ten steps noted above.

We can't totally fault it on engaging in joint ventures, though it could have done more of them, especially in the systems area. Many big companies would score as badly as Xerox, if not hit all ten. . . . Decline feeds on itself and organizations get into almost defensive postures. We're not saying it's easy to avoid these mistakes. . . . For far too long, managers have been terrified of breaking out of their old molds. Well, they can't sit around much longer and watch their companies dissolve before their eyes.

It's high time that you find a new approach to improving your performance, productivity, and profitability.

This action guide presents a powerful integrated approach to help companies solve their near-term problems, which could make all the difference in their ability to survive and thrive. It describes in depth the management options and issues facing companies in today's competitive business climate, and then provides several chapters that outline the necessary action steps you can take to keep your business vital.

It presents benchmarks that help businesses understand what their customers want and what their competitors are doing better. It shows how to evaluate products and processes and reengineer them for near-term improvements. It also explains how to rationally assess the pros and cons of downsizing, bring products to market cheaper and better, effectively encourage worker involvement, reward performance, and enhance communication between personnel on all levels.

From benchmarking performance, to reengineering products and processes, implementing continuous process improvement, and creating flexible organizations, this book shows managers how to take immediate action in almost every element of their business. In today's environment of slow growth and global competition, each manager or enterprise needs the important competitive edges found in *The Survival Factor*.

CAN YOUR BUSINESS SURVIVE?

To survive in the national and global marketplace, your business must adapt quickly in the near-term (the next twelve to eighteen months) to the new performance challenges. Your ability to respond effectively to changing business conditions is of critical importance to your survival.

George B. Bennett, chairman of Symmetrix, Inc., approaches the issue of change with the assertion that "organizations don't change until external catastrophes bring them near the edge of annihilation. This is unfortunate, because at that point, they are usually low on cash resources and have cynical demoralized personnel." The key is to act now, rather than waiting until you are forced to change.

Change nearly came too late for Tenneco, Inc., the Houston-based diversified industrial corporation. Mr. Dana G. Mead, the company's president and COO, recalls, "We realized that at most, we had a couple of years to do something. Otherwise, the opportunities of the present would suddenly become our past." Mead's solution was to institute a results-oriented, policy deployment focused, initiative-based management style, "giving every employee a clear picture of the results we expected and their role in getting them, as well as an understanding of how those results affect the organization's overall performance." Without such an understanding, Mead warns, "empowerment becomes nothing less than anarchy, quickly creating frustrated and ineffective managers."

The success Tenneco realized with this strategy was nothing short of astounding: the company's operating earnings and quarterly income soared, driving its debt ratio sharply down. Tenneco rapidly became a darling of Wall Street.

For management, the fundamental challenges of the 1990s are to balance competing priorities, restructure to meet changing times, and ensure that the people element remains a centerpiece of any change effort. Easier said than done, though, since many traditional change and improvement techniques, implemented as single solutions, aren't producing improvements sufficient to help businesses remain out in front in their market areas in the 1990s and beyond.

To achieve a quantum leap forward, management is finding that it must begin by examining and understanding how your business today performs its work, what work it does, and how that work aligns with the business's strategic vision. It then looks at the systems—financial management, application of appropriate technology, production processes, human resources, and other elements—that affect your work. And it even looks forward, anticipating competitive changes—both external and internal—that will demand corresponding changes in the existing systems and in the type of work that is done, and how, and by whom.

You can start today to improve your performance by adopting the critical action practices, tailored to your own needs, discussed in this book. Major businesses, as described below, have implemented these ideas and improved their performance and profitability by focusing on customer satisfaction.

In the 1990s, Southwest Airlines has been the only major domestic carrier to show net operating profits. A short-haul, low-fare, no-frills airline, Southwest's operating principles are simple: hire, motivate, and pay skilled employees who care and give them the freedom to meet customer needs. The selection process is meticulous, but once aboard, employees are told, "Have fun, it's infectious." Passengers seem to agree. Southwest has shown profits in each of its twenty-plus years—with operating costs 25 percent lower than the industry average.

As the fast food business boomed, Taco Bell sales sagged. Backed by extensive customer research, management focused exclusively on what their customers valued. Any change that promoted customer service value received total management support. With operations, service delivery, and resource management linked to a service vision that put customers first, profits soared. Today, Taco Bell is the fastest-growing fast food chain in the world.

Ranked last in customer service by a *New York* magazine survey, Citibank rethought—and redesigned—its entire retail operation to deliver exemplary customer service. Extended service hours, enhanced product lines, personalized service and support—everything passed control to the customers. Between 1974 and 1991, profits grew seven times. Today, Citibank is the highest-rated consumer bank in New York City—by a wide margin.

A 40 percent loss in market share convinced Xerox that something had to change. Discovering that "very satisfied" customers are six times more likely to remain with Xerox than just "satisfied" customers, the company turned itself inside out to provide total customer satisfaction. It transferred ownership of the business to teams of frontline technicians, transforming the role of field service managers to service facilitators. After winning the Malcolm Baldrige National Quality Award, and many "very satisfied" customers later, market share is growing again.

Service Master has built a $2 billion housekeeping and custodial services business on the idea that work should convey meaning and dignity to the person performing it. To this end, management works continuously to improve materials, technology, and techniques that lessen the physical demands on employees, support their dignity, and make them more productive. Training and support programs focus not only on the best means to get the job done, but also on the value of that job to the institution in which the employee works.

Ritz-Carlton hotels have long set the standard for personal attention. But when Ritz began listening to individual guest preferences and put this customer preference information online, the company secured an even stronger competitive edge—unsurpassed personalized service. As they like to say, if you request rocks in your pillow at the Pentagon City Ritz outside our nation's capital, you'll be asked, when you visit the Boston Ritz, if you still want rocks in your pillow. Ritz's ability to gather, digest, and communicate guest information to properties worldwide is unmatched in the industry.

Sibson and Company surveyed business leaders and identified several critical success factors and management approaches that, if properly implemented, could improve your chances for business survival.[2] Figure 1.1 shows these critical success factors. This book produces a set of near-term action steps that addresses these critical success factors, and can help get you started now on improving your business, before you are forced to change! Each of these critical success factors is linked to action chapters delineated in table 1.1.

There is a clear lesson to be learned here. Without "senior management support, clear objectives, an identified need for

Figure 1.1   Change Management Conditions Critical to Success

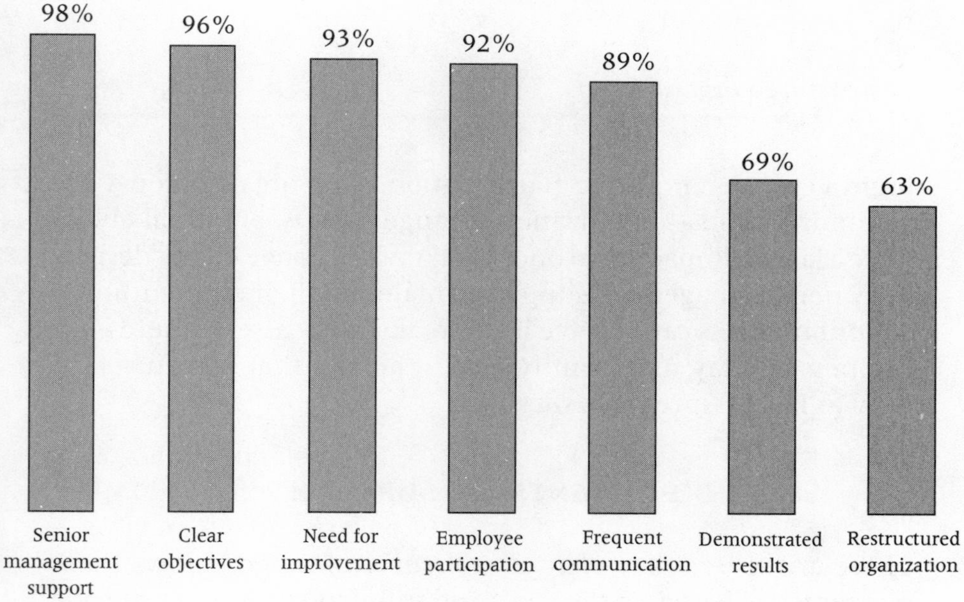

SOURCE: Sibson and Company, Inc.

Table 1.1   Crosswalk from Critical Survival Needs to Action Chapters

CONDITIONS CRITICAL TO SURVIVAL \ ACTION CHAPTERS	2 Plan	3 Survival factors	4 Benchmarking	5 Processes	6 Quality	7 Downsizing	8 Reengineering	9 Technology	10 Teams	11 Pay	12 Action steps
Senior management support	X	X	X	X	X	X	X	X	X	X	X
Clear objectives	X	X	X	X	X	X	X		X	X	X
Need for improvement	X	X	X	X	X	X	X		X		X
Employee participation				X	X		X		X	X	X
Frequent communications		X		X	X				X		X
Demonstrated results	X	X									X
Restructured organization						X	X				X

improvement, employee participation, and organization-wide communication—organization change efforts are unlikely to have a lasting impact. And once under way, change efforts desperately need management support to maintain their momentum.[3]"

Your business can survive if you realistically assess where your business is today, and identify specific actions that you must take now to help assure your survival.

ELEMENTS OF SURVIVAL

There are several key elements of survival noted below. These elements are based on the trials and tribulations your peers have experienced in their battles for survival. These insights are aimed at helping you come to terms with the scope of change required to assure your survival.

1. Pain and crisis should be expected. Do not wait until you are forced to change to begin your business self-assessment and survival actions.

2. Most businesses don't understand what their customers really want; therefore, they are doing a poor job in preventing loss of existing business to new competitors or they lack effectiveness in growing their business by attracting new customers. Customer satisfaction is critical to your survival.

3. Change is extremely difficult. If you have been producing a product or service for twenty-five years, it is difficult but necessary to modify the attitude of your personnel to encourage change rather than fear it. Successful change efforts must be based on providing your employees a clear and compelling reason *why* change is required for their survival.

4. Management leadership is the critical element in sustaining change. Managers must lead the change effort in every action and in every word spoken to your employees. No leadership, no change.

5. It is much harder to change the culture of your business than it is to change your management tools and techniques. To change your culture, you must have significant input and involvement by those responsible for effecting the changes.

6. Quality improvement (customer satisfaction) must become the mind set of every one of your employees, including yourself.

7. To survive, you must cut out every non-value-added product, service, or person. You must understand, simplify, or eliminate all of your unnecessary business processes, and eliminate redundant tasks and layers of supervisory inaction.

8. Develop a plan of action, tailored to your unique business situation, that you can live with. Your plan should provide a consistent vision and plan of attack that every employee can understand and participate in.

9. Your employees are the key to survival. Support your "survivors" or they won't stay the course with you. Talk with everyone to help your employees buy in to your vision for survival.

10. In the near-term, build practices that encourage productivity improvement, but remember that your approach to management and productivity improvement should encourage the continuous improvement of your business.

CHANGE TO SURVIVE

Your plan of action must be based on your own unique business situation. In order for you to develop an effective survival strategy, you must focus on core business problems that you face today. It is often surprising to business executives that a two-day tour of their operation by an outside consultant, talking with your people, can identify 80 percent of the problems that need to be addressed today. For you to provide a successful and lasting survival strategy that transforms your organization, you will need to implement the following.

- Develop clear goals and provide a strategic framework and plan of action to encourage and support change.

- Once your goals and vision are formulated, you will have to examine and select the various management options noted in chapters 3 to 12, and tailor the selected options to meet your unique business needs.

- ❑ Act to implement the policy deployment changes and management initiatives throughout your business.

If your business is to survive, you will have to lead the change process. Successful businesses at the turn of the century will focus on:

- ❑ Customer satisfaction (quality products and services).
- ❑ Cheaper, better, and faster response to internal and external customer needs.
- ❑ Faster-paced creation and innovation for new products and services.
- ❑ Significant productivity improvements to improve profitability.
- ❑ Flatter, less hierarchical management structures.
- ❑ Team performance versus individual performers.
- ❑ Policy deployment to every individual.
- ❑ Integrated information systems.
- ❑ Decentralized, smaller, autonomous business units.
- ❑ Smaller niche markets.
- ❑ Strategy-driven performance measurement.
- ❑ Flexible, better-trained employees.
- ❑ Sharing with employees the rewards of success.

To survive, you will have to encourage your team to embrace change rather than fight it.

Table 1.2 identifies the key management approaches or techniques presented in this book, and rates on a high, medium, or low scale the degree of difficulty that is involved to implement these management concepts in typical business organizations.

OPTIONS FOR ACTION

The action steps prescribed in this book concentrate on changing your way of doing business, and achieving improvement in your bottom line performance measures during the next twelve to eighteen months. Some of these initiatives, such as continuous process improvement, culture change, and quality improvement, will produce near-term benefits, but you will have to "stay

Table 1.2 Difficulty to Implement Change Index

MANAGEMENT APPROACHES/ TECHNIQUES	DIFFICULTY TO IMPLEMENT		
	HIGH	MEDIUM	LOW
Encourage leadership		X	
Cut costs—improve value	X		
Improve customer satisfaction	X		
Benchmark your performance			X
Adopt total quality management		X	
Implement continuous process improvement			X
Build teams		X	
Downsize operations		X	
Reengineer business	X		
Apply appropriate technology		X	
Adopt broad banding		X	
Pay for performance	X		
Pay for learning			X

the course" to gain the full synergistic benefit from some of these actions. Do not fall prey to the management consultants who want to milk dry the quality and culture change opportunities by encouraging you to spend more, and more for extra training and advice. Bring the implementation of quality and culture change into your management team and place the responsibility to improve business performance results on your own employees.

In order to support your action to change the way your business performs, you also need to be aware of the positive and negative aspects of adopting new management approaches that can help you survive the competitive pressures each of us faces. Table 1.3 illustrates the positive and negative aspects of change related to total quality management, customer satisfaction, role of leadership, team building, continuous process improvement, cost cutting, downsizing, reengineering, etc. Hopefully, this information will help you understand the potential and problems that can be encountered, and help you avoid the pitfalls.

JUST DO IT!

Action speaks louder than words. The near-term call for action by successful business leaders is "Just do it!"

The balance of this book is presented in a series of chapter modules that you can review and implement the suggested management techniques that will help your business improve productivity, performance, and profitability. Chapter 2 helps you develop your own survival plan by delineating the key management concepts necessary for survival and also presents an eighty-five-question self-assessment to help you determine what steps need to be addressed for your survival. Chapter 3 describes the ten key survival factors that can be implemented in the near term. Benchmarking, as described in chapter 4, can help you determine if you are really the best, what your customers' needs really are, and what your competitors are doing better than you are. Both radical

Table 1.3 Positive and Negative Aspects of New Management Approaches

NEW MANAGEMENT APPROACH	POSITIVE ASPECTS	NEGATIVE ASPECTS
Leadership	• Provide goals and vision • Continuous communication and inspiration forcing change	• Leadership by directive or policy statement doesn't work • Continuous action required
Cost cutting	• Reduced overhead and operational costs • Lean operation • Meet competitive value pressures	• Cut rather than growth strategy • Overdone, cut muscle rather than fat
Customer satisfaction	• Retain and expand customer base • Build brand loyalty • Link employees to customer response	• None
Total quality management	• Systemwide approach to improve customer satisfaction • Near- and long-term benefits • Improved reliability and value	• Can become a "training program" • 30 percent failure rate • Piecemeal selection of tools and techniques
Continuous process improvement	• Focus on understanding your processes • Step-by-step improvement of business processes	• Piecemeal small steps of change versus radical change

Table 1.3 (Continued)

Team building	• Share experience to better solve problems • Build employee morale • Enhance communication	• Teams' goals become focal point for action versus strategic goals • Small process improvement emphasis
Downsizing	• Smaller, flatter organization • Rapid cost-cutting tool • Near-term positive blip in stock value	• Reduces employee morale and trust • Not clear if longer term financial impact positive
Reengineering	• Understand business activities and processes • Simplify, reorganize for lean operation • Improve customer satisfaction by providing better value	• 70 percent failure rate • Lack of support for drastic change by leaders • Viewed as emergency solution
Broadbanding	• Increased operational flexibility • Simpler pay range system	• Fewer step pay increases for employees
Pay systems	• Pay for improving performance • Pay for learning • Increase productivity	• Some employees earn less than expected • Fairness of pay systems questioned

business process reengineering and continuous improvement are linked to understanding your business activities and process. Chapter 5 provides a seven-step process improvement methodology and describes process mapping techniques. Chapter 6 provides seventeen action steps to reduce your rework, and improve customer satisfaction by implementing total quality management. The agony of the downsizing trend is described in terms of the NYNEX Corporation experience, and supported by suggestions on how to downsize your business when necessary. How to reengineer your business enterprise, products, services, and processes is described in chapter 8. The fundamental synergetic relationships between reengineering, total quality management, and process improvement are also described to improve your ability to select the appropriate course of action. Chapter 9 suggests that you examine, refine, simplify, and reengineer your processes before applying technology to solve your near-term problems. By the turn of the century, most businesses will be operated by teams. Chapter 10 tells how you can empower your employees and accelerate change by implementing high performance teams.

Revolutionary changes are coming to businesses in terms of broadbanding, pay-for-performance, and pay-for-learning human resource management concepts described in chapter 11.

An action guide for survival is provided in chapter 12, based on ten immediate performance improvement priority actions you can begin to implement now.

From benchmarking, your performance to reengineering your products and processes, effecting continuous improvement, and creating fluid organizations, this book shows you how to take immediate action in almost every corner of your business. In today's environment of slow growth and increasing national and global competition, every manager and enterprise needs to understand and implement the important competitive edges found in *The Survival Factor*.

CHAPTER 2

Develop Your Own Survival Plan

To survive, you must develop a workable plan of action. Bruce D. Henderson described in the *Harvard Business Review*[1] the strategic advantage gained by having a plan of attack:

> You need to deliberately "search for a plan of action that will develop a business's competitive advantage and compound it. For any company the search is an iterative process that begins with a recognition of where you are and what you have now. Your most dangerous competitors are those that are most like you. The differences between you and your competitors are the basis of your knowledge. If you are in business and self-supporting, you already have some kind of competitive advantage, no matter how small or subtle. Otherwise, you would have gradually lost customers faster than you gained them." The objective is to enlarge the scope of your advantage by developing your own plan of attack.

To survive, you must address your own unique business problems. Off-the-shelf, momentarily fashionable management tools or techniques cannot save your business. Today, we hear of reengineering, total quality management, teams, continuous process improvement, and downsizing.

One of the problems that many businesses face is narrowly focused vertical stovepipe fad-of-the-month *nonintegrated* attempts to improve productivity and profitability.

This chapter describes the key management concepts that must be combined to help you develop your own plan for survival. In addition to discussing these management issues, it provides an independent self-administered assessment survey that can help you determine if you and your business are in great shape or if you need to develop a survival plan.

As noted in chapter 1, this book concentrates on near-term action. Your survival plan must focus on turning your business around quickly, and it must also address the fact that the depth of change in your business adoption of new operational approaches will continue over a period of time. Therefore, you will need to stress near-term actions to assure survival and also to promote new levels of change in your longer-term plan.

Chapters 4 through 11 provide modules for specific areas of action to improve your business. Chapter 12 contains a set of near-term priority action steps and a cross-reference to each of those chapters in which detailed "how-to" information is provided. This matrix also helps show the interrelationships between downsizing and reengineering, total quality management and process improvement, etc.

Because your businesses are unique and at different stages of success, you will have to assess these management tools, evaluate both the positive and negative impacts in terms of your business, and then proceed to improve your business by providing an integrated plan for action.

KEY MANAGEMENT CONCEPTS FOR SURVIVAL

Often, managers new to the "Survival Revolution" have different approaches to identifying the critical core values that their business must focus on today. In order to improve our collective recognition of survival concepts, the following fundamental critical management practices should be understood. Together, these practices represent the underlying base for developing your own unique plan to assure your business survival. The core survival attributes include:

1. Customer-Driven Quality

Quality is judged by the customer. All service attributes that contribute value to the customer and lead to customer satisfaction and preference must be the foundations for your business survival. Value, satisfaction, and preference may be influenced by many factors throughout the customer's overall purchase, ownership, and service experiences. These factors include a relationship with customers that helps build trust, confidence, and loyalty. This concept of quality includes not only the service attributes that meet basic customer requirements, but also includes those that enhance them and differentiate them from competing offerings. Such enhancement and differentiation may be based upon new offerings, combinations of service offerings, rapid response, or special service relationships.

Customer-driven quality is thus a strategic survival concept. It is directed toward customer retention, market share gain, and increased sales. It demands constant sensitivity to emerging customer and market requirements, and measurement of the factors that drive customer satisfaction and retention. It also demands awareness of technology developments and computer information system technology, and rapid and flexible response to changing customer and market requirements (such as new

financial options and government changes in health care requirements).

Such requirements extend well beyond defect and error reduction, and reducing complaints. Nevertheless, defect and error
reduction and elimination are causes of dissatisfaction that contribute significantly to the customers' view of your product or
service quality. In addition, your business success in recovering
from errors ("making things right for the customer") is crucial to
building customer relationships and to customer retention and
referrals.

2. Leadership

A company's top management leadership must create a survival
attitude in terms of explaining in clear language to your employees the real-world problems your business is facing. You
must tell your people the hard truth, and inspire and encourage
their participation in the necessary changes to your business. You
cannot implement the changes necessary for survival by yourself. You have to define the strategic changes needed to survive,
and inspire, and encourage in every action you take to stimulate
high performance. In the downsizing of your operations, you
must support the "survivors." Reinforcement of the business
survival values and expectations requires substantial policy deployment, personal commitment, and involvement. The top
management and senior leaders must take a very active part in
the creation of survival strategies, new business systems, and in
radically changing your process methods for achieving excellence. You must guide all activities and decisions of the company
by fostering a hands-on approach for changing the strategies,
systems, and process methods needed to assure your business
survival. The senior leaders must commit to the growth and
development of the entire workforce and should encourage participation and creativity by all employees. This can be accomplished by your regular personal involvement in visible activities,

such as planning, communications, review of company performance, and recognizing achievement. The senior leaders serve as role models, reinforcing the core values and encouraging leadership in all levels of management.

3. Process Understanding and Improvement

Achieving the highest levels of competitiveness requires a well-defined and well-executed strategic approach for both near-term radical business process reengineering and long-term continuous process improvement. The term "continuous process improvement" can also refer to both incremental and "breakthrough" reengineering improvement. Reengineering is all too often viewed by management as a one-time quick-fix solution. But reengineering your products and processes must be revisited continuously, because your competitive position is also changing continuously. A focus on really understanding your processes and developing a realistic strategy for process improvement needs to be part of all survival plans for all work unit activities of your business.

Improvements may be of several types. They may: (1) enhance value to your customers through new and improved services; (2) eliminate facilities, product lines, and processes that are unnecessary; (3) reduce rework, errors, waste, and non-value-added costs; (4) improve customer responsiveness and cycle-time reduction performance; and (5) improve productivity and effectiveness in the use of all business resources. Thus, survival is driven not only by the objective to provide better product and service quality, but also by the need to be responsive and efficient—both conferring additional marketplace advantages. To meet all of these objectives, the process of continuous improvement must contain regular cycles of planning, execution, and evaluation. This requires a basis—preferably, a quantitative basis—for assessing your progress, and for deriving information for future cycles of improvement. Such measurement information should provide direct links between desired strategic performance and internal operations.

4. Employee Participation and Development

Your success in meeting performance improvement and business survival objectives depends increasingly on the quality of your workforce, as well as multifunctional work team involvement. The close link between employee satisfaction and customer satisfaction creates a "shared fate" relationship between your business survival and the fate of your employees. For this reason, employee satisfaction measurement provides an important indicator of your efforts to improve customer satisfaction and business operating performance. Improving your performance requires improvements at all levels within your business. This, in turn, depends upon the skills, learning ability, and dedication of the entire workforce. Companies need to invest in educational development and automation to properly support the workforce and also should seek new avenues to involve employees and sales associates in problem solving and decision making. Factors that bear upon the safety, health, well-being, and morale of employees need to be part of the business's continuous improvement objectives. Increasingly, training and participation need to be tailored to a more diverse workforce, and to a more flexible work organization.

5. Fast Response

Success in competitive markets increasingly demands ever-shorter service, product development, and production delivery cycles. McDonald's fast food currently serves a typical drive-through customer in less than a few minutes, and they believe that is too long. McDonald's is reinventing their operations by investing in new fast food processing work flows, locating the kitchen closer to the customer delivery windows and counters, and building new drive-through service window arrangements to shorten their order processing time to help assure they will continue to provide really "fast" food for their customers. Customers look at the time it takes for you to satisfy their needs as a key measure of quality service. Also, faster and more flexible response to customers is now a more critical requirement of business cash-flow management. Major improvements in response time often require work organizations, work processes, and work paths to be simplified and shortened. To accomplish such improvement, more attention should be given to measuring delivery time performance. This can be done by making sale response time a key indicator for work unit improvement processes. There are other important benefits derived from this focus: response time improvements often drive simultaneous improvements in organization, quality, and productivity. Therefore, it is beneficial to consider sale response time, quality, and productivity objectives together.

6. The Building of Quality Processes

To assure your survival, you should place strong emphasis on building quality into services and into the processes through which they are produced. In general, costs of preventing problems are much lower than costs of correcting problems that occur "downstream."

Consistent with the theme of reducing rework by designing quality into your products and services, you need to emphasize interventions "upstream" at the early stages in processes creation. This approach yields the maximum overall benefits of process simplification, process improvement, and corrections. Such upstream intervention also needs to take into account the company's suppliers.

7. Strategic Outlook

Assuring business survival today and achieving market leadership require a company to have a willingness to make consistent commitments to customers, employees, suppliers, and stock-holders. Your near-term (next eighteen months) planning needs to determine or anticipate many types of changes, including those that may affect customers' expectations for your products and services, new technological developments, changing customer market segments, evolving governmental regulatory developments, impact of downsizing on employees, or new business tactics by your competitors. Plans, strategies, and resource allocations need to reflect these commitments and encourage change. A major part of your near-term commitments and efforts to change your business relates to the inspiration and development of employees and development of new relationships with your suppliers.

8. Management by Fact

Pursuit of strategic survival goals and improved operational performance for your business requires that operational management decisions be based upon reliable information, data, and analysis. Facts and data needed for strategic survival improvement and process assessment are of many types, including: customer satisfaction analysis, product and service performance delivery, overall measurement of operational improvement, assessment of market changes, competitive benchmark comparisons, supplier involvement, employee relations, and cost reduction success.

You need to focus on more effective "analysis" in terms of evaluating the larger meaning from data to support better decision making in the near-term. Such analysis may entail using data to reveal information—such as trends, projections, and cause and effect—that might not be evident without analysis. Facts, data, and analysis support a variety of business purposes, such as planning, reviewing company performance, improving operations, and comparing company performance with competitors' or with "best practices" benchmarks.

A major consideration relating to use of data and analysis to improve performance involves the creation and use of performance indicators. Performance indicators are measurable characteristics of services, processes, and operations your business can use to evaluate and improve performance and to track progress. The indicators should be selected to best represent the strategic survival factors that lead to improved customer satisfaction and operational business performance. A system of indicators tied to the strategic customer and/or company performance requirements represents a clear and objective basis for aligning all activities of the business toward common goals. Through the analysis of data obtained in the tracking processes, the indicators themselves may be evaluated and changed. For example, indicators selected to measure product and service quality may be judged by how well improvement in quality correlates with improvement in customer satisfaction.

9. Partnership Development

You should seek to build internal and external partnerships or alliances to better accomplish your overall goals. Internal partnerships might include those that promote team cooperation. Agreements may entail employee development, cross-training, interdivision cooperation, or new work organizations, such as high performance work teams. Examples of external partnerships include those with customers, suppliers, education resources, and even government organizations.

An increasingly important kind of external partnership is the strategic partnership or alliance. Such partnerships might offer a company entry into new markets or a basis for new services. Partnerships should seek to develop both near-term and longer-term objectives, thereby creating a basis for mutual investments. Partners should address the key requirements for success of the partnership, channels of regular communication, approaches to evaluating progress, and means for adapting to changing conditions.

These generic strategic survival factor core issues form the baseline for the development of your own unique strategy to help ensure your business survival.

DO YOU NEED A SURVIVAL PLAN?

Are you a good leader; do you manage based on fact rather than seat-of-the-pants judgment; are you focused on satisfying your customers; are you really concerned about your people? These are some of the questions you should think about in regard to determining if you need a "survival plan." To help you assess your business and cultural attitudes, a brief survey is provided below to help you self-assess your business situation.[5] To complete this survey, simply read each question or statement and answer by checking either: _____Yes, _____Somewhat, or _____No.

Organization: _____

Evaluator: _____

Leadership

1. Have all of the executives in your organization received adequate training on customer satisfaction concepts and practices to assure quality?

    _____Yes   _____ Somewhat   _____No

2. Are all of your senior leaders visibly involved in the development of an effective customer-focused approach to assure your business survival?

    _____Yes   _____Somewhat   _____No

3. Do your senior leaders practice what they preach when it comes to applying the new management concepts being promoted by your business?

    _____Yes   _____Somewhat   _____No

4. Has a corporate customer satisfaction vision or policy statement been written that inspires and communicates your business near-term policy deployment goals to your employees?

_____Yes _____Somewhat _____No

5. Has this policy been effectively communicated to all of your employees in the business?

_____Yes _____Somewhat _____No

6. Does the customer satisfaction approach you have defined emphasize the need for near-term business process reengineering breakthroughs, stretch goals, and continuous process improvement for all functions in your business?

_____Yes _____Somewhat _____No

7. Have quality management and improvement responsibilities been clearly defined and communicated to all levels of employees?

_____Yes _____Somewhat _____No

8. Does the cost cutting and process improvement efforts currently underway focus on coordinated change between different functions and departments in your business?

_____Yes _____Somewhat _____No

9. Do you really believe in customer satisfaction or is it just given "lip service" in your business?

_____Yes _____Somewhat _____No

10. Does your management team allocate adequate resources (finances, people, time, equipment) to the changes required to assure your survival?

_____Yes _____Somewhat _____No

Information and Analysis

11. Does your business collect and use quantifiable measurement data on all important dimensions of the products and services that you produce?

    _____ Yes   _____ Somewhat   _____ No

12. Are decision-focused data collected and reported on in all functions and departments in your business, including support functions such as administrative processes, accounting, marketing, etc.?

    _____ Yes   _____ Somewhat   _____ No

13. Does your business have ongoing methods for collecting and analyzing data on the views of your customers regarding the quality of your products/services?

    _____ Yes   _____ Somewhat   _____ No

14. Does your organization closely track and report all factors relating to the cost of poor performance (excessive scrap, high levels of rework, false starts due to inadequate planning, poor productivity, etc.)?

    _____ Yes   _____ Somewhat   _____ No

15. Does your business systematically analyze reliability and quality data in order to identify the causes of problems and identify process improvement strategies?

    _____ Yes   _____ Somewhat   _____ No

16. Does your business collect benchmark data from a variety of sources (customers, competitors, suppliers, etc.) to use in your strategic and functional planning process?

    _____ Yes   _____ Somewhat   _____ No

17. Does your business really focus on satisfying your customers by making quality a very high priority in the decisions it makes?

_____ Yes   _____ Somewhat   _____ No

Strategic Planning

18. Does your business collect and analyze quality-related competitive comparison data to develop your strategic plans?

_____ Yes   _____ Somewhat   _____ No

19. Does your business have operational near-term and strategic (two- to five-year) plans that describe overall business performance goals and strategies that all of your employees understand?

_____ Yes   _____ Somewhat   _____ No

20. Are employees, customers, and suppliers involved in the planning process?

_____ Yes   _____ Somewhat   _____ No

21. Are the near-term goals challenging, yet achievable, given your current business constraints?

_____ Yes   _____ Somewhat   _____ No

22. Has the customer satisfaction focus been well integrated into the general business planning being done in your company?

_____ Yes   _____ Somewhat   _____ No

23. Does your business have specific near-term improvement priorities and plans that have been developed by consensus (senior management and employee teams); and

have methods for monitoring these priority improvements been outlined in your plans?

_____Yes _____Somewhat _____No

24. Do process improvement plans include all functions within the organization?

_____Yes _____Somewhat _____No

25. Does your business have plans for ensuring that your suppliers are able to meet your performance requirements?

_____Yes _____Somewhat _____No

Human Resource Utilization

26. Do you have a corporate plan for your employees to play an active part in defining and developing new methods to improve your business operations and processes?

_____Yes _____Somewhat _____No

27. Are employees (team members) involved with the review and/or hiring of co-workers, as part of your employee selection systems to assess job transfer candidates or new employees?

_____Yes _____Somewhat _____No

28. Are quality and productivity criteria included and measured in the performance evaluation of every employee in your business (including senior management)?

_____Yes _____Somewhat _____No

29. Does your business use effective and timely methods of communicating both positive and negative results in

reaching your business goals, and the reason for changes in policy and plans, to every employee in your business?

____Yes ____Somewhat ____No

30. Is there an effective system for communicating productivity improvement, process improvement, new ways to satisfy your customers, and related quality ideas and concerns to top management, and does management provide meaningful and timely action or feedback regarding these suggestions?

____Yes ____Somewhat ____No

31. Do employees believe in the seriousness of the process improvement or reengineering efforts in your business, rather than think it is just another passing fad?

____Yes ____Somewhat ____No

32. Do the informal measures of employee performance and the real priorities in the organization contribute to your process improvement efforts rather than detract from it?

____Yes ____Somewhat ____No

33. Is there a well-defined and successful system for involving all employees in the process improvement process, and is the trend of employee involvement improving?

____Yes ____Somewhat ____No

34. Does your organization have a structured approach for communicating your business's customer satisfaction and quality goals to all of your employees?

____Yes ____Somewhat ____No

35. Do you have data that show how well the employees are able to apply the process improvement knowledge and skills they've learned on their jobs?

____Yes ____Somewhat ____No

36. Have all levels of employees (including top management) spent adequate time understanding the techniques and principles of process improvement?

_____Yes _____Somewhat _____No

37. Does your organization have an incentive or recognition program for rewarding employees for their productivity and process improvement efforts?

_____Yes _____Somewhat _____No

38. Do employees believe that your reward and recognition program is fair and that the awards are an adequate reflection of the effort and work they put into attaining them?

_____Yes _____Somewhat _____No

39. Do supervisors and managers make frequent use of informal nonmonetary awards or recognition for the productivity and process improvement efforts of their own subordinates?

_____Yes _____Somewhat _____No

40. Does your organization collect data and show a trend of improvement in the areas of employee morale, absenteeism, turnover, safety, grievances, and employee compensation?

_____Yes _____Somewhat _____No

Quality of Products and Services

41. Does your organization use a systematic process such as quality function deployment to define customer requirements and expectations?

_____Yes _____Somewhat _____No

42. Does the organization use a systematic and effective process for translating customer requirements into near-term operational requirements in each phase of the new product or service development process?

      ____Yes ____Somewhat ____No

43. Does the organization use a systematic and effective process for translating customer requirements into the planning process to improve existing products or services?

      ____Yes ____Somewhat ____No

44. Is there an effective system for disseminating information on business objectives and customer satisfaction requirements to your staff responsible for new product or service development?

      ____Yes ____Somewhat ____No

45. Is there evidence of the use of analytical techniques such as Pareto analysis, statistical process control, Taguchi method, cause and effect analysis, failure analysis, and so forth, for new product or service development?

      ____Yes ____Somewhat ____No

46. Does a system exist for assuring that planned performance requirements are functionally integrated into the product or service systems?

      ____Yes ____Somewhat ____No

47. Does your business use analytical (modeling, simulation) and/or physical/chemical measurement methods to measure all important performance expectation characteristics of your products and services?

      ____Yes ____Somewhat ____No

48. Does your company employ the latest state-of-the-practice technology in order to improve your performance?

_____ Yes _____ Somewhat _____ No

49. Is there an auditing process that is used to periodically evaluate the effectiveness of your management system?

_____ Yes _____ Somewhat _____ No

50. Does your organization employ adequate means of evaluating the extent to which the company's quality performance requirements are met?

_____ Yes _____ Somewhat _____ No

51. Does your business have plans and evidence of how you have worked with suppliers in a collaborative fashion to improve quality and related performance attributes?

_____ Yes _____ Somewhat _____ No

52. Does your business thoroughly apply quality management techniques in support departments such as research and development, administration, accounting, human resources, marketing, and others?

_____ Yes _____ Somewhat _____ No

53. Are the audit procedures thorough and free from bias, and do they reveal relatively few variations from standards?

_____ Yes _____ Somewhat _____ No

54. Has your business done a thorough job of documenting all important process information relating to your products and services?

_____ Yes _____ Somewhat _____ No

55. Are these documents all kept up-to-date and easily accessible?

_____ Yes _____ Somewhat _____ No

Performance Results

56. Is your business among the top 20 percent in satisfying your customers for your products/service?

_____ Yes _____ Somewhat _____ No

57. Is your organization among the top 20 percent in your market when it comes to product/service reliability?

_____ Yes _____ Somewhat _____ No

58. Has your company shown steady improvement in product/service quality over the last two years?

_____ Yes _____ Somewhat _____ No

59. Has performance been improving over the last two years in the areas of product recalls or service corrections?

_____ Yes _____ Somewhat _____ No

60. Are the data on your level of customer satisfaction collected in a thorough and objective manner?

_____ Yes _____ Somewhat _____ No

61. Is there a comprehensive system for assessing the performance level of products and services before and after they are placed in use?

_____ Yes _____ Somewhat _____ No

62. Has there been a steady improving trend in the reduction of the amount of scrap, rework, and rejected products/services during the last two years?

_____ Yes _____ Somewhat _____ No

63. Have data on scrap and rework been correlated with quality requirements so that appropriate interventions can be identified?

_____Yes _____Somewhat _____No

64. Does your business show quantifiable improvements in the quality of work performed by support departments such as research and development, administration, purchasing, accounting, and marketing?

_____Yes _____Somewhat _____No

65. Does your business have data to demonstrate quality improvements in goods and services provided by outside suppliers?

_____Yes _____Somewhat _____No

66. Does your business keep track of statistics on claims, litigations, and customer complaints and report these data to the appropriate personnel?

_____Yes _____Somewhat _____No

67. Has there been a steady decrease in the number of claims, litigations, and customer complaints over the last two years?

_____Yes _____Somewhat _____No

68. Is your business among the top 20 percent in your field when it comes to minimizing warranty or field support work?

_____Yes _____Somewhat _____No

69. Is the trend over the last two years showing a steady decrease in the amount of warranty or field support work?

_____Yes _____Somewhat _____No

70. Has your business shown any unique innovations, developed significant new products or services, or put in place any significant management changes that have positively impacted market share or income over the last two years?

_____ Yes _____ Somewhat _____ No

Customer Satisfaction

71. Do your customers believe that your products or services meet advertised performance specifications and provide them with a fair value for the price?

_____ Yes _____ Somewhat _____ No

72. Does your business have an overall high level of customer satisfaction with your products/services?

_____ Yes _____ Somewhat _____ No

73. Are measures of customer satisfaction accurate, objective, reliable, and complete?

_____ Yes _____ Somewhat _____ No

74. Are measures of customer satisfaction correlated with customer requirements and expectations?

_____ Yes _____ Somewhat _____ No

75. Has the trend in customer satisfaction data over the last two years been improving for your business?

_____ Yes _____ Somewhat _____ No

76. Does your business consistently rate higher than 80 percent of your competitors in customer satisfaction with your type of products and/or services?

_____ Yes _____ Somewhat _____ No

77. Are the comparisons the result of independent surveys conducted with a large sample of customers over the last two years?

_____ Yes _____ Somewhat _____ No

78. Is the trend in the data on your customer satisfaction compared with the competition improving over the last two years?

_____ Yes _____ Somewhat _____ No

79. Does your business have an effective process for handling customer service concerns and complaints?

_____ Yes _____ Somewhat _____ No

80. Do customers believe that you have an efficient and effective means of handling their problems and complaints?

_____ Yes _____ Somewhat _____ No

81. Do the data relating to customer problems systematically get fed back to the appropriate functions in your business, so as to improve your product or service quality?

_____ Yes _____ Somewhat _____ No

82. Do policies, procedures, and job definitions in your business empower customer contact employees to resolve complaints in a timely manner?

_____ Yes _____ Somewhat _____ No

83. Does your business have product and/or service guarantees that customers believe are superior to your competitors?

_____ Yes _____ Somewhat _____ No

84. Do you do an exemplary job of following through on written or implied warranties of the products and/or services you offer to customers?

_____ Yes _____ Somewhat _____ No

85. Do you employ any unique or innovative approaches to assessing customer satisfaction in your business?

_____Yes   _____Somewhat   _____No

How to Score Your Self-Assessment

❏ Score 5 points for each question you responded to as "Somewhat" on questions 1–70.

❏ Score 10 points for each question you responded to as "Somewhat" for questions 71–85.

❏ Score 10 points for each question you responded to as "Yes" for questions 1–70.

❏ Score 20 points for each question you responded to as "Yes" for questions 71–85.

Add all the scores to come up with a total. A perfect score would be 1,000 points.

Interpreting Your Score

Use the scale below to determine what your score means.

❏ 800–1,000 points: Your business should be a really successful operation.

❏ 600–799 points: You should be able to work successfully on the areas needing improvement so that your business can continue to perform above average.

❏ 400–599 points: You are operating below your potential, and you should develop and implement your survival strategy now.

❏ 399 or fewer points: You have a great deal of work to do to assure the survival of your business. It is not too late, but time is running out!

This questionnaire is simply designed to give you an idea of the survival factors that you should examine in more detail, so you can plan for process improvements now, rather than being forced to change, when it may be too late.

YOUR PLAN OF ATTACK

The reality today is that we must embrace change rather than try to find new excuses to avoid it. As Peter Drucker has said, "Every organization of today has to build into its very structure the management of change." It has to learn to ask, every few years, of every process, every product, every procedure, every policy, "If we did not do this already, would we go into it now, knowing what we now know"? And if the answer is no, the company has to ask, "And what do we do now?" It has to do something, not just conduct another study. Increasingly, companies will have to plan abandonment rather than try to prolong the life of a relatively successful policy, practice, product— something that so far only a few large Japanese companies have faced up to.[2]

The ability to create new products faster, cheaper, and better has to be built into the organization. According to Peter Drucker, each company has to build into its very fabric three systematic practices:

> First, each company requires continual improvement of everything it does. Every company will secondly have to learn to exploit, that is, to develop new applications from its own successes. Again, Japanese businesses have done the best job in this so far, as witness the way in which the Japanese consumer electronics manufacturer has developed one invention, the tape recorder. Third, you will have to learn how to innovate—and to learn innovation can and should be organized as a systematic process.[3]

Then, of course, one comes back to the beginning and the whole process starts all over again.

The bottom line is that we must change. We must aggressively plan for our survival today, to ensure our business survival in the global marketplace of tomorrow.

Your plan of attack should be based on the ten key survival factors identified in chapter 3. Your plan must be simple in terms of your vision, goals, and near-term action steps. And it must be optimized to meet your own specific near-term survival problems. As Dwight D. Eisenhower, architect of the Normandy invasion, once said, "Plans are nothing; planning is everything."[4]

CHAPTER 3

The Ten Key Survival Factors

To determine the ten key survival factors, the positive and negative aspects of near-term business improvement has been examined in more then 136 large, medium, and small businesses. The following set of survival factors, in some cases, would seem to be common sense advice to assure your business survival. However, it is surprising the number of business leaders who believe "all is well" and that change in the way they do their business is not needed. At a recent meeting at IBM of more than four hundred senior managers from around the globe, Louis Gerstner, the chairman, announced the results of an internal IBM survey that showed that 40 percent of their managers were not yet convinced that change in the way IBM competes was needed: "If that's so, he advised, don't stick around."

The old way of doing business is radically changing in every business enterprise. The ten key survival factors are delineated in table 3.1.

Table 3.1 The Ten Key Survival Factors

Survival Factor 1.	Demonstrate your leadership.
Survival Factor 2.	Stop the bleeding.
Survival Factor 3.	Cut your costs.
Survival Factor 4.	Satisfy your customers.
Survival Factor 5.	Do it right the first time.
Survival Factor 6.	Reengineer your business processes.
Survival Factor 7.	Rebuild your team.
Survival Factor 8.	Walk the talk.
Survival Factor 9.	Continue to improve.
Survival Factor 10.	The KISS factor.

DEMONSTRATE YOUR LEADERSHIP

Leadership is not easy to define. In *The West Point Way of Leadership*, a consultant explained West Point's unique approach to leadership this way: "At every *Fortune 500* institution in America, people are taught ethics. At West Point, people are taught character."

"Leader of character" is the phrase the Academy uses to describe the kind of leader it wants its cadets to become. A leader of character has all of the qualities we normally associate with leaders—ambition, confidence, courage, intelligence, eloquence, responsibility, creativity, compassion—and one thing more that we unfortunately overlook too frequently among civilian leaders: a leader of character is absolutely trustworthy, even in times of great stress, and can be depended upon to put the needs of others, the organization, above personal considerations—not now and then, or when the spirit moves him or her, or when it will look good on their résumé, but in every instance. Maybe the leaders at West Point know something that may sound paradoxical: rules—especially the rules of leadership—set the stage for initiative, loyalty, and teamwork of a highly powerful nature.[1]

Masao Nemoto, managing director of Toyota, spearheaded many of their efforts to develop new leadership and management initiatives. He found that managers often had personal styles that conflicted with the goals of the organization. To counter this, he wrote down his principles of management and distributed them to his associates whenever he took a new position. These principles were compiled by a number of managers at Toyota and are now called *The Sayings of Nemoto*. Here they appear condensed from an English translation by David Lu.[2]

Use these leadership principles, as Nemoto does, to let your employees know the principles that will be used to judge performance. Most turnaround or survival programs, from in-house establishment of total quality management to process improvement programs, focus on lower-level employees. Nemoto focuses on upper-level employees. Nemoto's sayings are a useful checklist for managers who want to make sure their leadership and the leadership of their associates further their survival initiatives. Most of these principles can be generalized to other management problems and programs, providing guidance and ideas for good leadership in any context.

1. *Improvement after improvement.* Managers should look continually for ways to improve the work of their employees. They should create an atmosphere conducive to improvements by others.

2. *Coordinate between divisions.* Managers of individual divisions, departments, or subsidiaries must share responsibility. Nemoto offers this advice to his managers: "One of the most important functions of a division manager is to improve coordination between his own division and other divisions."

A corollary of this is that upper management should not assign important tasks to only one division.

3. *Everyone speaks.* This rule guides supervisors of process improvement at Toyota, ensuring participation and learning by all members.

4. *Do not scold.* This is an alien concept to most Japanese managers. At Toyota, the policy is for superiors to avoid giving criticism and threatening punitive measures when mistakes are made. This is the only way to ensure that mistakes will be reported immediately and fully so that the root causes (in policies and processes) can be identified and amended. Assigning blame to the "messenger of bad news" clearly discourages reporting of mistakes and makes it harder to find the underlying cause of a mistake, but it is still difficult to train managers to take this approach.

5. *Make sure others understand your work.* An emphasis on teaching and sharing information is important because of the need for collaboration. At Toyota, managers are expected to teach associates about their work so that collaboration will be fuller and more effective.

6. *Send the best employees out for rotation.* Toyota has a rotation policy to train employees. There is a strong tendency for managers to keep their best employees from rotation. But the company benefits most in the long run by training its best employees.

7. *A command without a deadline is not a command.* This rule is used to ensure that managers always give a deadline or schedule for work. Employees are instructed to ignore requests that are not accompanied by a deadline. The rationale is that without a deadline, tasks are far less likely to be completed.

8. *Inspection for quality is a failure unless top management takes action.* The idea behind this is that management must prescribe specific remedies whenever a problem is observed or reported. Saying "Shape up" or "Do your best to solve this problem" is ineffective. So is failing to take any action once a problem is defined.

9. *Ask subordinates*, "What can I do for you?" At Toyota, this is called "creating an opportunity to be heard at the top." In your survival initiative, managers hold meetings in which employees brief them about their progress. Three rules guide these informal meetings:

a. Do not postpone the meetings or subordinates will think their project is not taken seriously.

b. Listen to the process, not just the results, since change must focus in on the process.

c. Ask the presenters whether you can do anything for them. If they ask for help, be sure to act on the request.

This philosophy can be generalized. If top management is perceived as willing to help with problems, employees are more optimistic about tackling the problems and will take management's goals more seriously.

No matter if you are trying to cut your cost, improve the quality of your products or services, or dramatically change your process by reengineering, without consistent leadership, your effort will fall short of your vision for changing your business.

STOP THE BLEEDING

Traditional cost cutting may not be sufficient to assure your business survival. You may need to sell off major businesses, close divisions or special facilities, or eliminate marginal product lines. This is one area in which executives have greater flexibility in taking decisive action in the near-term. Before you can proceed to adopt total quality management, reengineer your business, or improve the relationship with your employees, you must first bite the bullet and become a very "lean" organization.

In *Control Your Destiny or Someone Else Will*,[3] which describes Jack Welch's management revolution at General Electric, it was noted that he "moved quickly and aggressively . . . on taking the fat out of the bureaucracy, downsizing, and divesting businesses in which General Electric couldn't win, and investing where he thought they could win." His principal strategy was to be number 1 or 2 in any General Electric business area, and to get there by fixing, closing, or selling each of General Electric's businesses.

General Electric developed a business assessment matrix, shown in figure 3.1. The General Electric matrix is based on a large number of factors to measure variables. And because it uses

Figure 3.1   General Electric Business Assessment Matrix

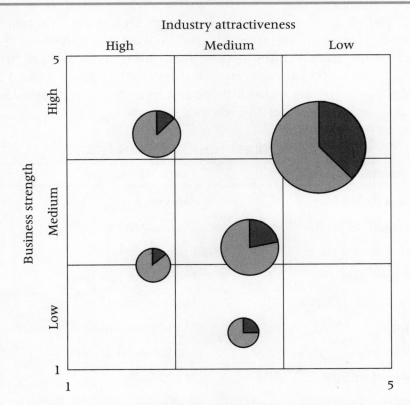

SOURCE: General Electric, developed by William Rothschild at General Electric, and consultant Mike Allen of McKinsey and Company. Also refer to *Strategic Alternatives: Selection, Development and Implementation*, by William E. Rothschild, AMACOM, 1979.

multiple factors, it can easily be adapted to the specific interests of management or the requirements of different industries by changing the factors and their emphasis.

The matrix is drawn by identifying critical internal and external factors, then weighting these to create measures of business strength (internal factors) and market attractiveness (external factors). The following provide a step-by-step approach to develop your own matrix. It is important to define the unit of analysis carefully before starting to collect data. Focus on meaningful strategic business units and define markets carefully.

1. Define factors. Select the important factors for evaluating business (or product) strength and market attractiveness. In General Electric's terminology, business strength factors are "internal" and market attractiveness factors are "external." Table 3.2 provides a list of factors to guide your selection (you may want to drop some of these and add some of your own).

Table 3.2 Internal and External Assessment Factors

INTERNAL FACTORS	EXTERNAL FACTORS
Advertising	Sales cycle
Breadth of product line	Demographics
Customer service	Entry barriers
Distribution	Environmental issues
Financial strength	Exit barriers
Image	Market concentration/structure
Management strength	Market-growth rate
Manufacturing	Market size
Market share	Political issues
Marketing	Profitability
New product development	Regulation

INTERNAL FACTORS	EXTERNAL FACTORS
Perceived quality	Resource availability
Repair and support	Social issues
Sales force	Technological advances

This step is very important—if key factors are overlooked, the analysis will not be valid. Trivial factors should not be included because they will sidetrack the analysis and waste time. A team can be used to identify factors, perhaps through the use of brainstorming techniques.

2. Assess the impact of external and internal factors. Starting with the external factors, review the list and rate each factor according to how attractive or unattractive it is. Use a five-point rating scale as noted below:

   a. Very unattractive.

   b. Unattractive.

   c. Neutral impact.

   d. Attractive.

   e. Very attractive.

Now, for the internal factors, do a similar rating using the following scale:

   a. Severe competitive disadvantage.

   b. Competitive advantage.

   c. Equal to competitors.

   d. Competitive advantage.

   e. Severe competitive disadvantage.

3. Assess the importance of external and internal factors and develop summary measures of strength and attractiveness. Now that you have established a rating for each factor, you need to decide how important each factor is to a general assessment of your business's position. Rank the factors by importance, placing the most important at the top of the list. Next, multiply each factor's ranking on the 1 to 5 scale (from step 2) by its importance weight.

4. Plot the business on your own matrix similar to the layout in figure 3.1. Now take the overall score of the business for each group of factors and plot it on the matrix.

5. Interpret the matrix. The strategic implications of the matrix for your survival planning are presented in table 3.3.

This approach can also be used to forecast the industry attractiveness and business strengths of your business units. The main focus is for you to develop a consistent basis to assess all of your key business units so that you can fix, close, or sell nonperforming operations to gain substantial financial and market improvement in the near-term.

CUT YOUR COSTS

The third key survival factor is for you to examine and cut every non-value-added cost in your business.

Reduction and control of your costs, especially overhead costs, are major challenges facing your business. Since this book does not focus on accounting practices, you may want to refer to the Ernst and Young *Guide to Total Cost Management* for detailed cost management techniques. Major changes are under way tied to process understanding, focus on cutting costs for staff, administration, and other overhead costs; and use of new accounting techniques, such as activity-based costing.

Table 3.3 Strategic Business Options

INDUSTRY ATTRACTIVENESS	BUSINESS STRENGTHS	SUGGESTED STRATEGIES
High	High	Grow Seek dominance Maximize investment
Medium	High	Identify growth segments Invest strongly Maintain position elsewhere
Low	High	Maintain overall position Seek cash flow Invest at maintenance level
High	Medium	Evaluate potential for leadership via segmentation Identify weaknesses Build strengths
Medium	Medium	Identify growth segments Specialize Invest selectively
Low	Medium	Prune lines Minimize investment Position to divest
High	Low	Specialize Seek niches Consider acquisitions
Medium	Low	Specialize Seek niches Consider exit
Low	Low	Trust leader's statesmanship Focus on competitor's cash generators Time exit and divest

Implementation of total cost management expands the traditional role of cost accounting and financial management. It takes your business from a preoccupation with labor costs to a broader view that includes return on quality (ROQ) cost elements.

SATISFY YOUR CUSTOMERS

The most important determinant of customer satisfaction is doing the job right the first time. This goal dictates "good" design, engineering, manufacturing, sales, and service practices for the business you are in. In a complex production/distribution chain, where everyone from manufacturer to retail clerk must always perform competently, problems will occur, even in the best-managed companies.

Such problems are costly, both to the company and the customer. When they occur, effective complaint-handling practices are required to maintain satisfaction. For a complaint-handling system to be effective, it must: (1) solve the individual consumer's problem, as well as (2) identify and correct the root cause of the problem. Thus, effective complaint handling is fundamental feedback necessary for doing the job right the first time.

The National Consumer Survey found that nearly one-third of those customers interviewed had experienced at least one significant problem during the year preceding the survey. Of those reporting problems, more than 60 percent reported financial losses averaging $142. Nearly 15 percent of the problem households reported lost time from work (e.g., waiting for repair people) in resolving their most serious problem. Other studies supports these findings. One found that approximately one out of four purchases resulted in some type of problem experience.

The fact that so many dissatisfied customers believe "It's not worth the effort" to complain or "No one would do anything" to resolve their problems suggests consumer pessimism.

Unfortunately, this pessimism may be well founded. More

than 40 percent of the households experiencing consumer problems were unhappy with the action business took to resolve their complaints. Those problems causing the greatest financial loss to the customer had the lowest satisfactory resolution rates.

A study conducted for Coca-Cola, U.S.A., validates the relationship between customer satisfaction and brand loyalty. Customers whose problems were not resolved satisfactorily reported a 25 percent repurchase intention. The brand loyalty of those customers who felt the corporate response was acceptable was 62 percent, and jumped to 94 percent for those customers whose problems were resolved to their satisfaction.

Other industry-specific research concerning large-ticket durable goods, financial services, and automotive services shows the same relationship between customer satisfaction and brand loyalty. These findings demonstrate the marketing advantages of an effective customer-complaint-handling system. To maximize the marketing benefits of effective customer complaint handling and to improve your customer satisfaction:

1. Solicit complaints. As a general rule, the brand loyalty of customers who experience problems increases when they complain.

2. Design corporate complaint-handling policies to optimize customer satisfaction in order to create the highest levels of continuing brand loyalty.

Your peers who have implemented customer satisfaction complaint-resolution techniques are gaining market share and providing a unique competitive advantage for their products or services.

Quality begins and ends with your customer. The customer indicates the right thing to do, and then the company has to find the right way to do it. As the supplier of a service, Federal Express is famous for doing whatever it takes to satisfy their customers.

Federal Express's team recognizes who their ultimate customer is and knows how important it is to meet their customer's needs. However, team members also need to recognize and meet the needs of their internal customers—other Federal Express employees with whom they exchange information, products, and services every day. All of us have people who depend on us for products or services to do their jobs, and each of you depends on services or products from others in order to do your job.

To make the work process flow smoothly and deliver a quality product to external customers, Federal Express also builds positive working relationships with its internal customers. This can be accomplished by asking three questions:

- What do you need from me?
- What do you do with what I give you?
- Are there any gaps between what I give you and what you need?

The answers to these questions are the key to "doing right things right."

DO IT RIGHT THE FIRST TIME

Providing excellent product and service quality has already become a key to success in the new competitive market. The level of quality expected by many customers continues to increase as leading competitors raise their standards of quality. In response to the demand for higher-quality products and services, a number of businesses have adopted total quality management systems.

The increasing importance of quality has been highlighted in some studies of quality management efforts. Examples of these results follow.

The Conference Board, Inc., a New York–based business research group, surveyed senior executives at eight hundred large U.S. corporations about their quality management practices.[4] Of 149 firms that responded, 111 reported that they had a quality management program in place. Thirteen of the remaining 38 said they were planning to institute total quality management. Sixty-two respondents reported that they measured the impact of quality on profitability. Of these, 47 reported "noticeably increased" profits due to quality management.

The Conference Board also interviewed senior quality executives at twelve American companies recognized for the excellence of their products and services and found that total quality management is the "strategy of choice" for assuring the economic position of American firms in the global marketplace.

PIMS Associates, Inc., a subsidiary of the Strategic Planning Institute in Cambridge, Massachusetts, maintains a proprietary database of twelve hundred companies and studies the impact of product quality on corporate performance.[5] PIMS researchers found the following:

1. Product quality is an important determinant of business profitability.

2. Businesses offering premium-quality products and services usually have large market shares and are early entrants into their markets.

3. Quality is positively and significantly related to a higher return on investment for almost all kinds of products and market situations.

4. A strategy of quality improvement usually leads to increased market share, but at a cost in terms of reduced short-run profitability.

5. High-quality producers usually can charge premium prices.

General Systems Company, Inc., a prominent management consulting firm in Pittsfield, Massachusetts, maintains a proprietary database for its clients, which shows that firms with quality management systems in place consistently exceed industry norms for return on investment. This higher return on investment was attributed to three factors.

1. Quality management can improve the quality of your products and services and reduce the direct costs associated with poor quality: inspection, rework, warranties, etc.

2. Improvements in quality tend to lead to increases in productivity.

3. The combination of improved quality and increased productivity leads to increases in market share.

The Union of Japanese Scientists and Engineers published a study by Dr. Noriaki Kano and others on the Japanese companies that won the Deming Prize between 1961 and 1980.[6] The study considered the earnings rate, productivity, growth rate, liquidity, and safety of the companies, and concluded that most companies either had an upward trend in business performance or were maintaining a favorable level. A few companies showed a temporary upturn in performance, then maintained a performance level above the industry average. When companies have pursued a vigorous total quality management program to improve their competitive capabilities, they often find that their profitability increases and their survival potential radically improves. American companies are accepting the view of quality that the Japanese learned from Kaoru Ishikawa and Americans such as Dr. Deming and Dr. Juran. The view of quality as a driver for competitiveness improvements has now gained acceptance in America. Quality is no longer seen as something to be added onto a product, or something achieved through inspection at the end of the line. Quality is now seen as a driver for achieving lower costs and shorter delivery schedules. Your competitors report that improving quality allows them to eliminate many inspections, reduce scrap and rework, improve performance and reliability, reduce unit as well as life cycle cost, and increase profits.

Chapter 6, entitled "Don't Do It Again and Again," provides extensive information that you can apply to your business to implement total quality management. Chapter 4, "Benchmark Your Performance," and chapter 5, "Understand Your Business Processes," support the development of your own total quality management initiative.

REENGINEER YOUR BUSINESS PROCESSES

Reengineering as characterized by enterprise-wide downsizing, as described in chapter 7, is an exercise in pain and suffering. In the 1980s, management consultants in droves advised companies to downsize. Unencumbered by a huge payroll, the lean corporation would be tough and competitive—at least in theory.

Leaders across the country still ponder the ever-elusive question: How can we regain our competitive edge? Enter Michael Hammer and James Champy, and a radical idea they call "reengineering." They've put their notions into a book entitled, *Reengineering the Corporation: A Manifesto for Business Revolution.*

Instead of restructuring by selling assets and making blind (cut ten to twenty percent of your employees or costs) head count reductions, Hammer and Champy advocate redesigning work around a company's business "processes"—those end-to-end activities that create value for customers. For example, at IBM Credit, the subsidiary that finances the parent company's computers, management has cut the credit approval process from six days to ninety minutes—simply by having one employee handle each financing request from beginning to end, rather than handing off a customers credit approval from department to department. Reengineering has helped many other companies, including Hallmark Cards, Aetna Life & Casualty, Bell Atlantic, and Texas Instruments, to reap similar improvements in performance, in processes as varied as new product development and customer service.[7]

Most businesses are fundamentally ineffective. Work is fragmented by task. All the marketing people are grouped in one department, and all the accounting people are grouped in another, and so on, whether or not they're working on the same project. This method is too error-prone, too expensive, and too slow. It's not designed to change. But when companies organize their work around a business process, they become much more effective. For example, if your business needs to reengineer your product development, the goal of reengineering in this case could be to try, as a starting point, to cut product development cycles in half. For example, cutting your cycle time from six years to three years.

These improvements are not accomplished by making people work harder or faster. These results are achieved by changing the process as described in chapter 5. Why does product development take so long? Well, marketing comes up with an idea and hands it off to engineering, engineering will say it can't be done and will throw it back to marketing, and so on.[8] And when the design leaves engineering for manufacturing, it must wait for the redesign needed for the product to be built. There are huge amounts of wasted time. But when you get the key people to work together—in teams, as described in chapter 10—and scrap the red tape, you can design and launch a new product much more quickly.

If you create a reengineering environment that supports integrated product development, significant cost savings can occur in the following areas:

- Costs reduced by eliminating non-value-added efforts:

   Thirty to 80 percent in business processes.
   Twenty-five to 65 percent in manufacturing.

- Cost avoidance/reduction due to process improvements:

Early production engineering changes reduced 50 percent.

Three times fewer product prototype models.

❑ Reduced costs during fabrication, manufacture, and assembly.

Twenty-three to 40 percent reduction in rework in manufacturing.

Costs reduced by simplification, parts reduction, and inventory control.

❑ Twenty to 60 percent reduction due to product and process simplification.

Since reengineering is about process, the very first thing you have to do is identify your company's processes (see chapter 5), which is not as simple as it seems. Most companies don't think in terms of process, but rather in terms of function. They think vertically instead of horizontally about the activities in their departments, not about the cross-functional collection of activities that create value. So, first, you have to identify your processes and give them names. Then you have to ask yourself questions like: Which of these processes are the least competitive? Which processes do my customers complain about? Which of them are costing me the most money, in terms of overhead?

For all the talk about reengineering, only about 5 percent of American businesses are implementing enterprise-wide reengineering as defined by Dr. Hammer. Another 10 to 15 percent are selectively reengineering their products or services. In too many cases, businesses claiming to have jumped on the reengineering bandwagon are just paying lip service, because it is the trendy management concept.

Many of the early reengineering case studies are from companies that were forced to change their management approach in order for their businesses to survive. The impact of radical change on an organization and the management team is extremely stressful and the transaction is very difficult.

If you are forced to change, now is the time to reengineer your processes. The approach recommended is to focus on better process development by understanding, simplification, and changing your individual processes. Look for the bottleneck problems identified as part of your competitive benchmarking assessment (chapter 4). As leader, you will have to establish near-term critical priorities for action. In other words, is your immediate problem lack of desired products, poor reliability or quality, or excessive costs? Address the critical bottleneck problems first.

Reengineering of your products or processes stresses taking a new look at the outcomes your business process needs by starting your reengineering effort with a clean sheet of paper. The goal is cheaper, better, faster, simpler processes. Chapter 8 describes in detail how you can reengineer your products and processes.

REBUILD YOUR TEAM

If you are fighting for your survival, you need to inspire, encourage, support, and rebuild your team of co-workers. Teams are hot, and they may be the productivity improvement breakthrough of the 1990s. By the turn of the century, most American businesses will have adapted teams or multifunctional teams as described in chapter 10. Businesses like yours are using teams to break down the communication barriers between departments, bring new products and services to market faster, improve their quality, and provide better value to their customers. Executives, middle managers, white-collar and blue-collar administration and factory workers, and even the union members, are supporting the use of teams.

As described in *Fortune* magazine, multifunctional teams were few and far between in the late 1980s.[9] Only a handful of companies—Procter & Gamble, Digital Equipment, TRW—were experimenting with them. However, today, those business leaders who have already taken the plunge and adopted multi-functional teams have seen impressive results:

- At a General Mills cereal plant in Lodi, California, teams schedule, operate, and maintain machinery so effectively that the factory runs with no managers present during the night shift.

- At a weekly meeting, a team of Federal Express clerks spotted—and eventually solved—a billing problem that was costing the company $2.1 million a year.

- A team of Chaparral Steel millworkers traveled the world to evaluate new production machinery. The machines they selected and installed have helped make their mill one of the world's most efficient.

- 3M turned around one division by creating cross-functional teams that tripled the number of new products.

As one of the key survival factors, we encourage the empowerment of your employees by adapting multifunctional teams. However, teams are not for everyone. "They make sense only if a job entails a high level of dependency among three or more people. Complex manufacturing processes common in the auto, chemical, paper, and high-tech industries can benefit from teams. So can complicated service jobs in insurance, banking, and telecommunications. But if the work consists of simple assembly-line activity like stuffing pimentos into olives, teams probably don't make sense. Says Edward Lawler, a management professor at the University of Southern California, "You have to ask, 'How complex is the work?' The more complex, the more suited it is for teams."[10]

In addition to creation and use of multifunctional teams, if you have downsized or embarked on an aggressive reengineering effort, you will need to focus on helping the "survivors" in your business. Chapter 10 provides more details on how to support and empower your team.

WALK THE TALK

Your business survival depends on your people more than anything else, and people lead or are led—they are not managed. Survival depends on effective leadership, and you must provide that leadership. By taking the initiative, providing an example, and showing the way, you can lead your subordinates and inspire your peers to follow you almost anywhere. Top leadership is essential, but leaders are needed at all organizational levels. Effective leadership does not necessarily depend on your place in the organization but rather on your enthusiasm and your visible commitment to the process of improvement.

Building awareness—understanding what must be done to survive—is important to you and your business. Every person in the organization must become aware of the need to improve, of the promise offered by change and their risks due to inaction. Awareness of the seriousness of your business situation by your team is the key that opens the door to the potential of improvement.

As you work on building awareness throughout your organization, begin to establish lines of communication both horizontally and vertically. Honest, open communication is probably the single most important factor in successfully creating a new environment. It will take time, but it can lead to trust and mutual respect. Sometimes, it may be the only thing that keeps your survival effort alive. If people keep talking to one another, they can work through problems, overcome barriers, and find encouragement and support from others involved in your change efforts.

Constancy of purpose establishes a common direction for all organizational elements and ensures that efforts at all levels contribute to achieving broad objectives relevant to the entire organization. Communicating your vision of the organization's goals and objectives throughout the company is essential to focusing improvement efforts for the common benefit. Your behavior and attitudes must reinforce this constancy of purpose. You must do what you say you are going to do to be believed and supported by your team.

Employees who trust their managers and who are trusted and respected in turn can provide the edge that organizations need to provide superior services or products. Workers have the best, most up-to-date knowledge about how well processes are working, what problems have arisen, and how things could be better. If their opinions are respected, they will share their knowledge and creativity with management—the only way to ensure improvement.

Trust and respect are essential for individual participation. Without such an atmosphere, people will not take action or make recommendations they perceive to be risky to themselves. Change is a process that depends on every person being unafraid to take chances and not worried about risking self-esteem. You must be open and honest with your people and establish channels of communication that are reliable and accessible to everyone. If people broach ideas, they should be praised; if they identify problems in the process or system, they should be thanked; when they contribute, they should be recognized; when they fail, they should be supported; and when they succeed, they should be rewarded. As their leader, you must create an atomosphere of trust and support, and you are responsible for maintaining each individual's sense of self-worth and self-esteem, even in difficult times.

Success should be rewarded, and chapter 11 describes the essentials for paying for skills and knowledge as part of your survival strategy.

CONTINUE TO IMPROVE

By making continuous improvement a part of your daily routine, you will need to integrate it into all aspects of your work as described in more detail in chapter 5. Continuous improvement only approaches maturity when it is applied routinely to all of your organization's work. Routine application entails using the Plan-Do-Check-Act process improvement cycle in all areas; collecting data and using those data to assess process suitability, removing roadblocks to your improvement efforts and those of others, and continuously improving your knowledge and expertise. Ideally, continuous improvement should be your normal approach to doing your work; it must become your way of life.

Continuous process improvement is a never-ending effort. Perfection is an ultimate, unattainable goal, but its ideal is the basis for continuous improvement efforts. You must view everything your organization does in terms of interrelated processes. Process improvement should become your organization's way of life. Goals and objectives are realized through process improvement. Your own focus should be to improve all the processes you own and remove all those barriers under your control that hinder others from improving their own processes. The only true measure of your performance over time is the degree of process improvement you achieve.

Process standardization is a means of defining a process and ensuring that everyone understands and employs it in a consistent manner. It is difficult to improve something that is not well defined. Process standards communicate the current, best-known way of performing a process and ensure consistent process performance by a variety of individuals. With a standard, people have a way of knowing that they are doing their jobs correctly, and *you* have a means of assessing their performance objectively. Process standards provide the baseline from which to continuously improve the process. The people doing the work should maintain and update standards as they improve their processes so that the standards always reflect the current, best-known means of doing their work.

Your organization's ability to improve its processes depends in part on the inputs to those processes. To the extent that you procure materials and services from other organizations, your continuous improvement effort depends on those suppliers. Expanding your improvement culture to all your suppliers will help ensure that the quality of your process inputs is sufficient to meet your own improvement objectives. You can expand your culture of continuous improvement by working more closely with your suppliers, helping them get their own improvement efforts underway, building mutual trust and respect, and generally by becoming a better customer yourself.

In addition to operational process improvement, you will need to reexamine your investment and support of new technology and automation of those processes where it is beneficial. Chapter 9 shows that after you have simplified and reengineered your processes, you need to implement the appropriate level of technology to improve your productivity and competitive position. It is very important in the survival mode to avoid use of "too much" or "too little" technology to solve your problems.

THE KISS FACTOR

For businesses in the midst of major transformation efforts, it is very important to remember the KISS Factor. As in politics, we talk about "It's the economy, stupid"; in our efforts to survive, we admonish, "Keep it simple, stupid." Your plan of attack and your communication of the direction your team must go to survive ought to be simply elegant. You should synthesize and simplify your vision of what must be done in such a manner that *every* employee understands *why* you must change your operation, and *how* you plan to do it.

The hardest part for leaders is to determine what must be done now. There are so many conflicts, opportunities, and wrong paths that are offered; as a leader of your business, you must focus on and do the critical things.

To help keep things simple, you need to define your vision, goals, and plan of attack in the form of a realistic, usable, integrated plan of attack.

These ten key survival factors, and the following chapters, can help you develop a unique approach tailored to your business to help you survive.

CHAPTER 4

Benchmark Your Performance

ARE YOU REALLY BETTER?

Benchmarking can help you understand how well you are providing products and services to satisfy your customers, and what your competitors may be doing better than you. This comparison can show the gap in your performance and can provide an excellent management tool to help you to improve your performance. This chapter will focus on using benchmarking to help you break out of the "not invented here" syndrome. All too many companies look at their performance as above average and much better than their competitors, but, in reality, most companies do not really know how well they perform in comparison with their competitors. Only 35 percent of American businesses currently benchmark their competitive performance; therefore, most of us do not know if we are better than our competitors.

In a recent management assessment of a major insurance company, the corporate president conveyed a very positive attitude and fostered a feeling that the organization was the "best" in their business. Sorry to say, this executive did not know the gap between his performance and his competitors, who were improving their customer service and insurance product values. If you believe that you are perfect, with no opportunity or need to improve, you are on your way down the slippery slope of failure. Benchmarking your products and services can help make the case as to "why" you should change your business processes.

Managers who have used benchmarking to make major improvements in their work have found the following points to be very useful:

- ❏ Successful benchmarking depends on an ongoing commitment from senior management.

- ❏ Successful benchmarking is based on how well you know and understand how your own business processes are accomplished.

- ❏ Implementation of your benchmarking process depends on your willingness and ability to change your way of doing business and adapt to new competitive pressures.

- ❏ Realize that your competition is improving constantly, and that customer requirements will continue to become more demanding. Therefore, you need to anticipate future changes and plan on "shooting ahead of the duck."

- ❏ Competitors are more willing to share information than you might expect, but do not ask for anything that you are unwilling to share about your own business operations. Benchmarking networks are excellent starting points to facilitate your benchmarking efforts.

- ❏ The focus during benchmarking should be on the key enabling processes and practices as well as your performance measurements.

◘ In benchmarking, look for leading companies that compete in your business area, at companies in other industries that are recognized as leaders in your area of special interest, and at your own internal business units that are known to be effective in similar work.

BENCHMARKING AT XEROX

In the late 1970s and early 1980s, Xerox experienced many business survival problems that were compounded by the worldwide recession. They experienced market share losses; their financial performance began a serious decline; and they were faced with very strong competition from both Japanese and American copier companies.

The cost of doing business at Xerox was too high and the reliability and quality of their products and services were not high enough. Major changes in the way they managed their business and in the way they did their work were needed to meet the requirements of their customers.

In 1979, Xerox pioneered a management process they called "competitive benchmarking." Xerox's recent strong performance in regaining its competitive edge in the marketplace can be attributed largely to its benchmarking program. At first, only a few of the Xerox operating units used this process, but today benchmarking practices are used throughout Xerox. According to a *DataQuest* research newsletter:

> Xerox's benchmarking program deserves the lion's share of the credit for the organization's turnaround in recent years. A whole new way of doing business was inaugurated with the start of this program. Every group and system was dissected as Xerox searched for ways to become more competitive.

One of the first and most successful steps Xerox took to assure its survival and regain its competitive edge was to institute their benchmarking program. After studying the Japanese product development system (with the help of Xerox's Japanese partner, Fuji Xerox), Xerox began to revamp completely the way its products were designed. Xerox also established benchmarks for functional organization areas. For example, L. L. Bean served as a benchmark for shipping operations, and Sears, Roebuck & Company provided a model for the management of field distribution.

This chapter is based on the management leadership and competitive benchmarking process developed by Xerox. Xerox is the "best practice" model for benchmarking. Xerox has provided permission for inclusion in this chapter of material from their publications.[1,2,3]

WHAT IS BENCHMARKING?

Benchmarking is a straightforward dynamic management process adaptable to all functions of your business. It can be defined as "the continuous process of measuring your products, services, and practices against your toughest competitors or those companies known as leaders in their field."[4] Benchmarking is a structured approach for looking outside your organization (or, as Dr. Hammer, the reengineering guru describes it, "looking outside the box") by studying other organizations and adapting the "best practices" to improve your business and help assure your survival.

Your goal must be superiority in all areas—quality, product reliability, and cost. You can use benchmarking as a tool by which you can identify, establish, and achieve standards of excellence— standards based on the realities of the marketplace.

Benchmarking is a learning experience. You can observe what the competition is doing now and project that potential change in performance into the future. You should look at how they operate; and, where it makes sense, adapt and build upon their practices for your own use. Ultimately, benchmarking provides information that can help set your performance goals for attaining leadership, as well as developing and implementing action plans to achieve that position.

It is also important to understand what benchmarking is *not*. First, it is not simply a mechanism for determining "head count." You may find that the process results in a reassessment of assigned resources, but its aim is to ensure that your company survives the changing business climate and remains a competitive business.

Benchmarking is *not* a program, or campaign. It's not a one-time quick fix or a cure-all. It *is* an ongoing management process that requires constant updating and the integration of competitive information, practices, and performance into the decision making and communication functions at all levels of your business.

Benchmarking is the means by which you can establish continuously your priorities, targets, and practices that will lead to competitive advantage in the changing marketplace. Benchmarking is a survival strategy and not just a cost reduction effort. Benchmarking is a continuing process, not an end product.

THE BENEFITS OF BENCHMARKING

If you only look internally at your own current practices, you will never develop the best strategies to totally satisfy your customer requirements.

One of the greatest values of benchmarking is learning the practices that are used by your competitors and other companies to achieve their results. Some of the management benefits are:

- Benchmarking provides insights into new ways of doing business, and challenges "business as usual" methods.

- Benchmarking depends upon and builds effective teamwork through mutually established goals and the team's agreement to achieve them.

❏ Benchmarking provides an increased awareness of your costs and performance in products and services compared with those of your competitors.

❏ Benchmarking is a logical and proven method for developing survival strategies and achieving superior performance that will help your business survive and prosper.

Benchmarking should be a standard process used to evaluate your business success in meeting your customer requirements. The performance standard should be that each work function achieves and maintains superiority or, at the very least, parity in meeting the requirements of your customers in terms of quality, schedule, and cost performance. If each of your employees' efforts is not at the performance level of "best practice," your business will be less effective than your competitors'. Customer satisfaction can only be achieved by meeting your customer's requirements—that is, product features, level of service, quality, availability (schedule), reliability, price, value, reputation, and their prior experience with your business. These requirements constantly change and are influenced by the changes your competitors are making. If you think you are the best, but really don't know how your competition is performing, you are on your way to competitive suicide.

To meet the competitive challenge and respond to customer requirements, each of your business units should establish competitive benchmarks for their major functions, including gathering the necessary competitive data; establishing a process to update the data; projecting your best competitors' future performance; and taking the necessary actions to achieve and maintain competitive superiority.

Benchmarking can help reduce the cost of quality by identifying the best practices in any area of activity. It helps you to determine what the real requirements are. It can also be used effectively in problem solving and quality improvement projects.

The key ways benchmarking helps to improve your business are to:

- Identify your performance against competitive accomplishments in the context of changing customer requirements.
- Identify the right measurements against which you should judge your performance.
- Find ways to use the "best practices" to improve your performance, including the reduction of rework and prevention of errors.

As you involve more of your team members in solving problems in your business, benchmarking becomes a powerful tool for identifying problems, finding potential solutions, and identifying opportunities.

THE BENCHMARKING TEMPLATE

David Kearns (formerly president of Xerox) described their benchmarking process:

> We took Competitive Analysis one step further and came up with what we call competitive benchmarking. It's an intense, in-depth study of what we think is our best competition. It's a continuing, never-ending process, and it's an integral part of our emphasis on quality. Every department at Xerox should be benchmarking itself against its counterpart department at the best companies we compete with. We look at how they make a product . . . How much it costs them to make it . . . How they distribute it, market it, sell it and support it . . . How their organization works . . . What kind of technology they have. Then, we all go back and figure out what it takes to be better than they are in each of those areas.[5]

Simply speaking, benchmarking is the process of:

- ❑ Figuring out what to benchmark.

- ❑ Finding out what the benchmark is.

- ❑ Determining how it's achieved.

- ❑ Deciding to make changes or improvements in your own practices to meet or exceed the benchmark.

These four actions, while sounding fairly simple, require thinking and analysis. They require that you know your own business processes and practices down to the smallest detail, as described in chapter 5.

The Xerox benchmarking template, as shown in figure 4.1, is a 'guide, a template, or a pattern, for accomplishing the various analyses required for benchmarking. Unlike a process model, the

Figure 4.1　Xerox Benchmarking Template

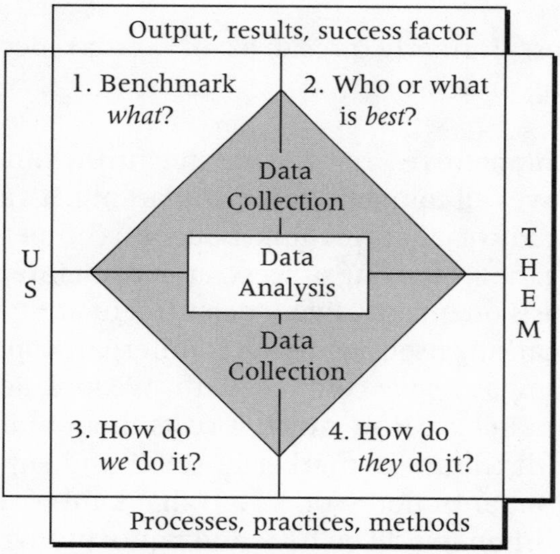

SOURCE:　Xerox Corporation.[6]

template is not strictly "sequence sensitive," nor does it focus on "actions to take." Rather, it poses four questions that might be answered in different sequences. "Us" and "Them"—notice the two vertical axes of the template. The two quadrants to the left pose questions about your results or processes (us); the two quadrants to the right refer to whom or to what you are making the comparisons (them). The "them" can be a competitor or another division within your business.

In the first comparison (tier 1), the template is cut in half horizontally, with the resulting two quadrants suggesting comparing outputs or results. To begin your reengineering comparison, you must answer the questions "Benchmark *what*?" and "Who or what is *best*?" In other words, what will you choose to compare yourself against? We will refer to this first comparison as the "upper-tier" comparison.

At the heart of the template is data collection and analysis. "Data" is just another name for "information." You will need to have a plan for collecting information both about yourself and about the object of your benchmark study. Naturally, you will need the information to be in a form that allows comparison.

If you went no farther than the top two quadrants, you would have accomplished a competitive analysis. You would know what the benchmark is today and how you measured up against it.

The lower-tier comparison is the comparison of the bottom two quadrants, which constitute true benchmarking—understanding the reasons for the differences and understanding what changes in process, practices, or methods must be undertaken to meet or exceed the benchmark.

Only the lower-tier study results will allow you to make changes toward improvement. Lower-tier questions address problems like: "*Why* are their results better than ours?"; "*How* do they achieve that better process?"; "Should we 'do it' completely differently?"—these are the questions that lead to radical change or continuous process improvement.

The objective of benchmarking is to change the way your

business views your performance, which should lead to significant improvement. Without change in processes, practices, and, ultimately, results, benchmarking is an incomplete academic exercise.

THE FIVE PHASES OF BENCHMARKING

The key steps in the benchmarking process are divided into five phases as shown in figure 4.2, starting with the planning phase and evolving through analysis, integration, action, and finally maturity.

In each of the five phases, there are actions that you need to accomplish, each of which is described below. While you can and should modify them to meet your particular environment, it is important to remember that these actions are minimal for successful implementation of the overall benchmarking process.

Planning Phase

The objective of this phase is to lay out your plan for benchmarking. The key questions you need to address are the basic elements of any plan. Specifically, three general questions must be answered:

First: What will be benchmarked? Every function of your business delivers a "product" in the broadest sense. It may be a service call, a functional service, financial report, or a hardware product. How well do you use your assets? The benchmarking process is equally applicable to all of these "products," so the first step is to identify your product or output.

Second: Who is the best competitor? While you recognize that your major business competitors are your primary concern, you can also benchmark against other companies that set the standard in a functional activity. For example, the Xerox distribution organization decided to benchmark its operations against those

Figure 4.2 Process Phases for Competitive Benchmarking

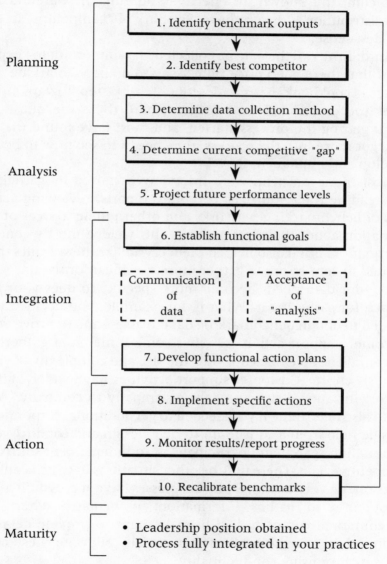

Planning

1. Identify benchmark outputs
2. Identify best competitor
3. Determine data collection method

Analysis

4. Determine current competitive "gap"
5. Project future performance levels

Integration

6. Establish functional goals

Communication of data

Acceptance of "analysis"

7. Develop functional action plans

Action

8. Implement specific actions
9. Monitor results/report progress
10. Recalibrate benchmarks

Maturity

• Leadership position obtained
• Process fully integrated in your practices

SOURCE: Xerox Corporation.[7]

of IBM and Kodak, who compete with them directly. But they also benchmarked some functions against L. L. Bean, the catalog sales company known for effective and efficient warehousing and distribution of its products. So think of "competitor" in the broadest sense.

Third: How will the data be collected? It is important to keep in mind that there is no one "right" way to do benchmarking. No standard cookbook exists to describe step-by-step how to implement the process. Most managers share the same questions about getting the process started, and most have found that as they got more into the process, they began to see how to better develop and implement it.

Most managers who were interviewed started by gathering and reading trade journals, corporate reports, reviewing activities of benchmarking networks and other public sources of information about their competitors. This yielded mostly general information, but it also helped them crystallize the specifics they wanted to zero in on, to gather more specific information.

As your data needs become more specific, so does your approach for gathering it. What if, for example, you decided you needed to obtain benchmarking data to assess and improve your customer support activities? After some initial data gathering, you would be able to "scope out" the size and complexity of your analysis effort. (Customer support activities have widely differing organizational structures from company to company.) You could also determine if you needed to get additional corporate or outside help from a consultant to help design and conduct your information search and participate as an independent source of competitive data. There may be other situations in which consultants can be very useful. Some businesses have successfully used consultants to gather information, particularly when the benchmarked company had been hesitant to provide detailed information. Consulting firms can usually alleviate these concerns by promising confidentiality.

Other businesses have found that direct contact with benchmarked companies is the best way, especially when there is a mutual exchange of information, or when the participating company receives a copy of the results. One caveat to this approach, however: carefully consider all of the strategic and proprietary security implications involved with exchanging your information. The message is that there are several methods for data gathering. Pick that method or combination of methods that best meets your unique needs.

Just as there is no one specific method of collecting competitive data, there is no one specific approach to measuring it. Typically, some business units started by benchmarking the factor of cost, applying such standard metrics as cost as a percent of revenue. See table 4.1 for other types of metrics used.

Table 4.1 Commonly Used Benchmark Metrics

Cost and Cost-Related Metrics

Percent of cost function to revenue:
  Sales
  Service
  Customer administration
  Distribution
  General and administrative

Labor overhead rate (percent)

Material overhead (percent)

Manpower performance ratio

Months of supply

Cost per page of publication

Cost per order

Cost of form processing

Cost per engineering drawing

Table 4.1 Commonly Used Benchmark Metrics (Continued)

Cost per change order

Occupancy cost as percent of revenue

Return on assets

Quality

Internal and external customer satisfaction results

Percent of parts meeting requirements

Percent of finished product quality improvement

Return on quality (ROQ) improvements

Rework rates

Defect rates

Billing error rate

Service

Work support ratio

$/SACAT hour (standard available call activity time)

Service response time

First-time fix of service call problem

Percent of supplies delivered next day

Percent of supplies delivered on time

Percent of parts available for the technical representative

SOURCE: Xerox Corporation[8]

Sources of competitive data are limited only by your imagination and creativity. They might include your own personal and professional contacts, trade associations, technical journals, or even advertisements. You can solicit information directly from the competitor or analyze its products. However, as you proceed, remember that you need not "reinvent the wheel." In many cases, other people in your business may already have the data, or have used a particular methodology for getting them, which you can use. The key sources of benchmarking information include your competitors. Also, industry leaders should be included in benchmarking studies if they have demonstrated expertise in a particular area. The review of other internal business organizations within your company should be viewed as information sources and can be useful in finding new ways to improve as well (e.g., measuring customer satisfaction). Studying only one company probably will not yield a benchmark. At least several companies should be studied for comparison and identification of the best practices.

Once the companies to be studied have been identified, information is available from a variety of sources. The following are the most common:

- Review of external reports, financial reports, professional publications, trade journals, magazine articles, market research results, government data, library materials, and media reports.

- Professional and trade association meetings and literature; trade shows.

- Personal contacts; other units; networking, corporate staff field personnel, employee involvement and quality specialists, and former employees regarding nonproprietary matters.

- Telephone and mail surveys.

- Direct company visits.

- Consultant studies and industry experts.

- Competitive product analysis.

- Customer feedback (often, this may be the most important, in that it signals a benchmarking study is needed to correct a problem or respond to changing customer requirements).

To facilitate benchmarking, use of a benchmarking network, such as the International Benchmarking Network, can
be used. This is a great opportunity for:

❑ Sharing experiences with the benchmarking process to improve skills and overcome barriers in furthering acceptance
and the successful use of competitive benchmarking.

❑ Exchanging information, sources, and successes to optimize
benchmarking efforts and avoid duplicating efforts and "reinventing the wheel."

❑ Providing a means for group problem solving of common
issues and a forum for dealing with interorganization issues
and dependencies.

❑ Coordinating benchmarking efforts with common competitors to maximize the investment of both your company and
competitors' efforts.

❑ Improving the understanding and documentation of the
benchmarking process.

❑ Assuring consistency of information and measurement criteria among organizations where beneficial.

Interestingly, many managers have found that competitors are
often willing and eager to share information—usually on a quid
pro quo basis. The results of a study can be provided to each
company in exchange for its participation. Recognizing the value
of the data to itself, one company even offered to help fund a
follow-up study.

Analysis Phase

Once you acquire the data, you must then analyze them. The
objective of this phase, after all, is to understand your competitors' strengths and to assess those strengths against your own
performance. It is therefore essential that you ask these basic
questions.

1. Is the competition really better? If so, how much?

2. Why are they better?

3. What can we learn from them?

4. How can we apply what we have learned to our business?

The answers to these and to other questions should help define the performance "gap"—negative or positive—between your competitor and yourself. You now have an objective basis upon which to act—to close a negative gap or extend a positive one.

But remember, too, that your benchmark is an ever-shifting target. You need to understand clearly not only where the competitor is today, but also where it is likely to be tomorrow. Try to develop analytical approaches and sources that can be kept current through periodic reviews. You must also assess your competitor's potential performance so that the dimensions of the gap can be projected over time. It is important, therefore, to collect the necessary data from readily updatable sources that will facilitate meaningful analysis now and in the future. Recalibration of your data is described in the action phase.

Integration Phase

Benchmarking really begins to "earn its keep" during the Integration Phase. You have acquired the hard data, which have revealed the areas to benchmark and then worked with them to determine the extent of the task. You are now ready to use these data to set your goals—to gain or maintain superiority and to weave those goals into your planning process.

But the first initiative in this phase is to gain senior management's acceptance of the results of the benchmarking analysis and its commitment to develop near-term useful action plans. This is essential to success, and it will require time. All of the managers interviewed stressed the importance of clearly and convincingly demonstrating the reliability of their benchmarking data. In all likelihood, the data will be questioned, particularly if they point to a significant negative gap. So make sure your methodology is sound.

Once senior management understands and accepts the data and your conclusions, the development of strategies and action plans can begin using the problem-solving process delineated in figure 4.3.

This is the time when the investigation of the practices of your competitors is so valuable. Acceptance of the effectiveness of your competitor is much easier to understand once you know the methods they have used to achieve their results.

Timing is essential. Data should be gathered, analyzed, and reported so that they can be included in your business's current planning cycle. Most companies view benchmarking data as essential to set long-term goals, which are based on competitive realities, determine strategies, and document those strategies in their business plans.

Figure 4.3 Problem-Solving Methodology

- **Identifying and Selecting a Problem**
  The senior management, or the benchmarking team, identifies critical business survival or process concerns that the problem-solving team shall focus on.

- **Analyzing the Problem**
  The benchmarking team determines what is wrong, gathers and interprets factual data, investigates possible causes, and zeros in on the problem. This includes establishing the requirements of a satisfactory solution in the form of objectives or desired outcomes, and noting any restrictions or limitations on a solution.

- **Generating Potential Solutions**
  Benchmarking team members "brainstorm" to generate as many solutions as possible, without restriction or prejudgment.

❑ **Selecting and Planning the Solution**
The benchmarking team evaluates the ideas and comes up with recommendations. Even though a proposed idea may not work by itself, it can have valuable elements. Time should be taken to combine the good parts of various ideas; each alternative should be carefully and critically evaluated.

❑ **Implementing the Solution**
The benchmarking and implementation team anticipates implementation problems, makes plans to include those whose support will be necessary, and assigns and accepts action responsibilities.

❑ **Evaluating the Solution**
The implementation and benchmarking team follows up later to determine whether the solution actually worked and takes any corrective action necessary.

Keep in mind, also, that benchmarked goals can be set at any and all levels of operation. For instance, your business could have as one of its overall goals an annual percentage increase in productivity. There are also operational objectives supporting the company's goals—specific targets relating to shipping accuracy, productivity, cost cutting, and operating budgets. This "cascading" of objectives downward to all levels ensures that each person clearly understands his or her role in meeting the overall business survival goals.

Finally, benchmarking needs to be clearly communicated, through formal action plans, down through the various business organizational levels.

As shown in figure 4.4, there are fifteen actions needed to fully integrate the benchmarking process into your business management process. There is a lot to be done during this phase, and it is essential that the major issues be addressed. Some of the questions that need to be answered include the following:

- Are specific, measurable goals and targets clearly established?

- Is the benchmarking process an integral part of the overall unit planning cycle?

- Have action plans been identified?

Figure 4.4 Fifteen Action Steps for Benchmark Integration

Step 1. Results of benchmarking are synthesized into proposed strategic goals for the organization.

Step 2. Findings and proposed goals are agreed to by top management and operating unit management; and the mission, goals, objectives, and operating principles are approved.

Step 3. The communication process is used to explain the need for changes, including discussions on building, understanding, and encouraging a commitment to change.

Step 4. Goals are integrated and published in the business plan guidelines and strategic direction.

Step 5. Specific business action plans are plan strategies and action plans are developed to meet these goals.

Step 6. The business plan is reviewed and approved by management.

Step 7. Operating unit priorities for operating plan are established, reviewed, and approved by operating unit senior management.

Step 8. Operating plan guidelines and targets are published along with priorities.

Step 9. Operating plan submission and reviews include plans to meet targets, describing status versus long-range goals and checkpoints for operating plan years.

Step 10. Final approval of operating plan establishes commitments for plans and target performance.

Step 11. Plan and target performances are incorporated into performance appraisal process.

Step 12. Review and measure near-term progress on implementation of plans and in meeting targeted performance.

Step 13. Special management steering committee meetings are held to review specific plans/issues, and decisions are reached and communicated.

Step 14. Recalibration of benchmarks is done as part of business plan update each year (repeat step 2 for goals).

Step 15. Progress reports are discussed with employees at least once a year.

SOURCE: Xerox Corporation.[9]

A checklist (see figure 4.5) has been developed for use by managers in reviewing their benchmarking process.

Action Phase

Having completed the Integration Phase, you now have a plan based on benchmarking data, and you've set specific, measurable goals and objectives that are incorporated into that plan. Additionally, these goals have been clearly communicated throughout the unit.

It is now time to implement your benchmarking plan and to periodically assess and report your progress in achieving it.

Businesses usually build into their plan certain milestones that trigger its updating. This updating may require the recalibration of the benchmarking data. Units have found oftentimes that this recalibration need not be as extensive as the original data gathering. It should, of course, be sufficient to indicate what is happening as a result of your actions. Obviously, it should also reflect what your competitor is doing.

Figure 4.5 Checklist for Managers

- ❏ Are benchmarking findings part of the proposed goals of your organization?

- ❏ Are organizational goals, incorporating benchmarks, published as part of the functional operating plans and strategic direction each year?

- ❏ Are there specific benchmarks in each function?
  Is there clear accountability for generating benchmarks and delivering against benchmark-driven targets?

- ❏ Are the benchmarks that have been chosen appropriate?

- ❏ Are the benchmarks supported by a full understanding of how the competitor does business?
  Are their competitive practices better, should they be emulated?
  Can we accomplish same or better results?

- ❏ What are the specific programs/actions to close the gap?
  Is the value of each action understood and quantified?
  Are program/action plan expectations realistic relative to value and timing?

- ❏ Are plans to meet targets, with current status, incorporated into all functional operations reviews?

- ❏ Are improvement plans and performance targets incorporated into performance appraisals?

- ❏ Are business goals and progress toward performance targets communicated and discussed regularly with all employees?
  Is value of actual results in terms of quality, schedule, and cost clearly documented?

- ❏ Is recalibration of benchmarks done on a regular basis?
  Has "best practice" competitor or function changed?

Likewise, a periodic updating of customers' satisfaction perceptions is needed. Use the appropriate number of measurement devices to track customer satisfaction, pinpoint problems, and establish benchmarking targets. These actions are designed to be *proactive* rather than *reactive* to customer perceptions. One way you can accomplish this is through customer opinion surveys, which regularly sample customer satisfaction, as described in chapter 6.

Finally, a reporting mechanism is needed, and progress reported to all employees. This information should be provided on a regular, recurring basis so that each person can see how they are doing.

The specific questions that need to be addressed in the Action Phase include:

- What are we accomplishing as a result of our plan?

- What are our competitor's current and projected strengths and weaknesses?

- What parts of our plan need to be readjusted?

- Is a recalibration process in place?

Maturity Phase

How do we know when our benchmarking process has reached maturity?

The answer is twofold: first, when you have attained a leadership position, and, second, when performance assessment and process change have become essential, ongoing elements of your business survival management process.

While you may not be the leader in all areas at all times, that should be your overall goal. Only through striving to achieve superiority in delivering reliable products and services to your customers in the most cost-effective manner can you achieve leadership in the marketplace and assure survival of your business in a fierce competitive marketplace. Benchmarking will have matured only when it has become an integral part of your overall management practices.

THE INTERNATIONAL
BENCHMARKING CLEARINGHOUSE

The International Benchmarking Clearinghouse is a service of the American Productivity and Quality Center. Founded in 1977, the center is a nonprofit organization that works with business, labor, government, and academia to improve productivity and quality.

The International Benchmarking Clearinghouse is an excellent source to begin your information gathering and networking effort for your benchmarking effort. The clearinghouse is designed to promote, facilitate, and improve benchmarking by helping your organization improve processes, locate others for benchmarking, and screen potential benchmarking partners.

A recent survey of organizations involved in benchmarking rated the following clearinghouse services of greatest benefit to them:

- ❏ Information searches and research.

- ❏ Benchmarking partner identification.

- ❏ Benchmarking training.

- ❏ Electronic network.

- ❏ Getting started in benchmarking.

- ❏ Database of past studies.

The clearinghouse offers your business the opportunity to learn how top companies survive in the changing global marketplace, adopt and adapt "best practices," and achieve breakthrough process improvement results.

Current special benchmarking studies are under way at the center on several topics, including:

❏ Quality of communications.

❏ Financial tools: a best practices study.

❏ The new product development process.

❏ National sales benchmarking.

❏ Needs assessment in the sales process.

❏ Customer call centers.

❏ Environment, health, and safety management processes.

For more information, contact:

American Productivity and Quality Center
International Benchmarking Clearinghouse
123 North Post Oak Lane
Houston, TX 77024
Phone: (713) 685-4666
Fax: (713) 681-5321

SUMMARY OF BENCHMARKING FACTORS

As a management process, benchmarking can be a critical tool to help you achieve your strategic business survival goals and objectives. It provides a disciplined, logical approach for objectively understanding and assessing your strengths and weaknesses by comparing your results with the best in your area. It causes the development, implementation, and updating of specific action plans designed to achieve success.

However, in order to become an integral part of your management process, benchmarking is ultimately dependent on two attitudes—management's backing and your flexibility and willingness to change. Key attributes include:

A Commitment from Top Management

When it comes to benchmarking your business performance, your management team must be behind you. Senior management must recognize the need for change and improvement. It must repeatedly demonstrate that it is willing to make the tough decisions needed for survival. It should commit your business to benchmarking as one of the primary means to help assure your survival.

A Willingness to Adapt

Probably the single most important factor for success in benchmarking is whether we as individuals are willing to learn from others. That means learning from other managers within your business and from managers in other companies.

You should be proud of your accomplishments. But you must understand that your company does not, and cannot, always have the best answer to every problem you encounter. You can and should learn from others and measure yourselves against the best that you can be—or be better than. By adopting this approach, and the rigorous application of benchmarking, you are taking a big step toward assuring your survival.

An Active Leadership

For you to implement the benchmarking process effectively, the benchmarking team manager must play a leading and supportive role in all stages of the effort. This is especially true in determining which companies will be benchmarked, how the information will be gathered, and who will be involved.

Benchmarking can be done by the team in one of two ways—

either as an employee involvement process improvement team or by selecting one or more individual members to do the investigation and present the findings. Regardless of the approach, the benchmarking team manager should make sure that all team members have a common understanding of the expected output and customer requirements.

If you are the benchmarking team's manager, you should be involved with the work to assure that requirements are understood and the plan of action has a high probability of success. This can be done by participating in periodic reviews of progress and suggesting alternative approaches. Ensure that the group has access to needed information and the resources necessary to complete the tasks. Assist where necessary to remove any barriers that impede progress. Keep all benchmarking team members informed and provide the opportunity to discuss and make recommendations as the work proceeds. Very importantly, let the team know you appreciate new and creative problem-solving approaches from the benchmarking team.

Effective use of the benchmarking process begins with an understanding of how it can be used to find ways to identify and effect improvements in functional performance and output results. The role of the benchmarking team manager in facilitating the team members' understanding of the process is very important.

In summary, benchmarking is management process for measuring your products, services, and practices against your best competitors in the areas of cost, quality, and reliability. Using your benchmarking data, you can develop plans and strategies to maintain positive gaps or close negative ones. You can measure your progress periodically, constantly updating your relative position. Your ultimate goal is superiority in all areas.[10]

Benchmarking results in specific performance targets based on what your competition is expected to do, rather than some manager's imprecise, intuitive estimate of what needs to be done. It is a rational way to establish near-term business survival objectives.

Ultimately, benchmarking reflects an attitude—an attitude characterized by your desire as individuals to constantly strive for excellence in everything you do.

This chapter on benchmarking provides another management tool to help you overcome the "not invented here" syndrome, and provides a more factual basis for demonstrating the need for you and your employees to change to beat the competition, and help assure your survival.

CHAPTER 5

Understand Your Business Processes

Both radical reengineering process improvement and continuous process improvement address the creation of positive change in the way your business functions. This chapter describes what you can do to better understand, simplify, and improve your processes, and ways you can map your process work flow.

DO YOU UNDERSTAND YOUR PROCESSES?

Unfortunately, most managers do not really understand their operational processes. All too often, managers believe they have the documentation, or seat-of-the-pants experience, that defines their business activity. However, when they sit down to describe or map their process flow, many managers discover problems, surprises, bottlenecks, and unneeded processes that are reducing their competitive position by adding time delays or excessive costs to business operations.

The benefits of process examination includes: simplification of process work flows, elimination of whole steps in your processes—enhancing the integration of your suppliers' role in your process improvement effort—elimination of non-value-added costs throughout your corporate process, and the reduction of variation that improves your quality.

A MODEL FOR PROCESS IMPROVEMENT

The process improvement model shown in figure 5.1 is a four-step cycle that begins with the activities needed to create an envi-

Figure 5.1   The Plan-Do-Check-Act Process Improvement Cycle

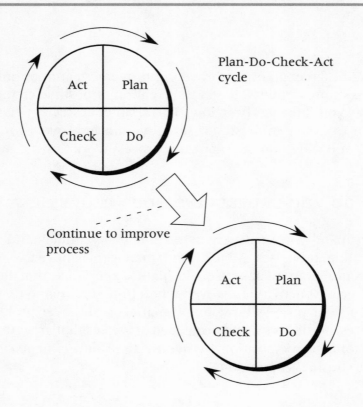

Plan-Do-Check-Act cycle

Continue to improve process

ronment conducive to process understanding by anticipating and planning for change, implementing change, checking your performance improvements, and continuing to improve your process activities. This improvement cycle is often referred to as the Plan-Do-Check-Act (PDCA) cycle for process improvement.

STEPS TO IMPROVE YOUR PROCESSES

The process improvement steps described below are based on *An Introduction to the Continuous Improvement Process—Principles and Practices*.[1] These seven basic process improvement steps are delineated in table 5.1.

Table 5.1 Process Improvement Steps

Step 1. Set the stage for process change.

Step 2. Select candidate product or process for improvement.

Step 3. Understand and define the process.

Step 4. Standardize the process.

Step 5. Change the process.

Step 6. Continue to improve the process.

Step 7. Assess process improvement performance.

Each of these seven steps is described in more detail below.

Step 1. Set the Stage for Process Change

At the organizational level, setting the stage for process change involves everything your business does to become aware of the need for significant change, and to establish a commitment to actually follow through by changing your processes. It includes goal setting, barrier reduction, training, and leadership. Setting the stage means that you must create an environment in which process improvement is encouraged and nourished. Management must have a clear vision of what it wants to accomplish and where it wants to go, and it must put in place support systems to help your employees implement process understanding and change.

At the team and the individual levels, setting the stage involves selecting the process improvement team(s). It requires additional training in process simplification concepts; new work-flow analysis tools, and techniques that you will need for the contemplated process improvement effort. The team(s) need to learn how to function in the changing overall organizational environment and support the individuals involved to accomplish their task.

Step 2. Select Candidate Product or Process for Improvement

The process improvement leadership and team members select the product and/or processes on which they will focus their process improvement effort. Selecting the process target involves identifying known problem areas that require immediate action, benchmarking industry process improvement opportunities, setting priorities, and choosing those process improvement efforts that present the most serious competitive problem or offer the most significant opportunity for business survival or improvement. Once the process improvement targets are selected, the process improvement teams must identify the major problems to be addressed and the level of change required (radical business process reengineering or incremental continuous process improvement). The process improvement team may, based on new data, revise their plan for improvement that builds on the team's objectives. Identifying measurement points, such as defects per million parts, cost targets, market share, or profit goals, is necessary before beginning the process improvement effort.

Step 3. Understand and Define the Process

Once the specific process effort has been targeted for improvement, the team should define the planned effort as clearly and completely as possible. Process improvement is based on determining your customers' needs, documenting how the process is currently performed, determining the type of change that is required, and identifying measures of process improvement performance. Documentation should be sufficient for the task and consistent among all organizational processes. A sound process definition provides a consistent base from which to begin change; without knowing where you are at a given moment, it is hard to determine how to get to your destination. A road map (process map) is needed to assure that vital steps have not been missed and to track the progress of change.

Step 4. Standardize the Process

By defining or standardizing the new improvement process, the team institutionalizes the current best way to perform the process. It also creates a tool for instructing people in their jobs within a consistent performance definition, it provides a framework for evaluating performance consistently, and it provides a basis for evaluating the success of the process improvement efforts. Process improvement team leaders ensure that their team members are trained to the new process standard, and help adopt its use. Once the new process standard is in force, teams can measure performance against that standard and respond appropriately to deviations from it to meet your new goals. The process standard should continue to reflect the best current way of performing the process for your business.

Step 5. Change the Process

Once a team has defined the process standard, it should optimize the process, and continue to significantly improve it. This effort should ensure that the process meets its stated and perceived requirements; adopts state-of-the-practice tools and techniques; encourages significant product and process simplification; eliminates unnecessary equipment and facilities; and establishes reliable, adequate data collection systems to improve your processes.

Step 6. Continue to Improve the Process

Continue your efforts to improve the process by following the Plan-Do-Check-Act (PDCA) cycle. Your process improvement effort should assure that your team(s) implement solutions, check for improvement, and act to institutionalize and continue the process improvements. The team's effort involves developing ongoing solutions that address your requirements and improvement goals. Data collection and performance measurement methodologies must support your process improvement actions. The process improvement team needs to be trained in the techniques necessary to carry out the plan.

Step 7. Assess Process Improvement Performance

As the team succeeds in its process improvement efforts, it should reassess their data to determine how well actual performance matches their performance improvement goals. Successful improvement should be institutionalized; less-than-successful efforts require another pass through the process improvement cycle.

After process improvement has been implemented, the process improvement team should document the improved performance. That documentation allows others to benefit from the lessons the process improvement team has learned and brings recognition for the team's efforts. It also provides a road map for replicating successful process improvement techniques. Documenting the improved process also requires the team to update its process definition, and requires that process goals to be redefined to reflect a new standard of performance. Recommending follow-up actions or subsequent process improvement actions is also useful.

No single correct formula or "canned" solution can be used to achieve process improvement in all situations or all businesses. A core set of ingredients, however, is evident in most successful process improvement efforts, and they can be applied to your own business.

Your process improvement effort will be unique in its details, but, in general, it should move your business toward satisfying the six criteria listed below.

1. Exceed your customer's requirements and expectations and be a high-quality supplier.

2. Support significant state-of-the-practice change-oriented management systems. Encourage process improvement change in every facet of your business.

3. Work to eliminate barriers that prevent people from having pride in their work, and involve everyone in your process improvement efforts.

4. Tap the power of individuals, multiplying that power through training and teamwork, and focus that power on process understanding and process improvement.

5. Make decisions based on data rather than on opinions or emotions; stimulate creative system thinking; and seek process improvement in products, processes, and services.

6. Adopt state-of-the-practice work flow analysis tools and techniques.

SIMPLIFY YOUR SYSTEM PROCESSES

The simplification of design and manufacturing processes, development of accurate process documentation, reengineering existing or creating new system processes, reconfiguring flow of materials and work to focus on the quickest path for action, and very careful analysis of design for manufacturing and assembly strategies produce significant benefits in terms of increased productivity, business profitability, and survival.

It is essential to distinguish between activities that make life easier, or enable your business to operate more smoothly, and those that really affect the value provided to the customer.

In *Dynamic Manufacturing*, Hayes et al., state:[2]

> For example, neither the flows of information within the factory nor material flows in and out of inventory generally create value for the customer. Only the conversion activities add value. Adhering to this principle means continually searching for ways to eliminate activities that do not add value (ranging from scrap and rework to parts waiting time to underutilized equipment and people), so that more of the factory's activities can be directed toward improving the products and services delivered to customers.
>
> Creating a factory that is a distinctive source of value for customers requires that process problem solving be pervasive. Its intent is to remove or reconfigure those things that hinder the creation of value. The factory, therefore, must be willing and able to change process conversation steps, setup procedures, and plant layouts as opportunities to enhance value added and to reduce waste are identified. What goes on in the factory is not cast in concrete but is continually being modified.

To simplify your product and process systems designs, the process improvement team must first understand the customer's real requirements and priorities. When resolving and placing priorities on requirements, the customer and developer must define and evaluate trade-offs. For example, what are the operational environments and performance levels that are an absolute necessity for this product?

There are an interminable number of questions relating to the system trade-offs between product performance/reliability, cost, and timing/schedule. In the ideal scenario, there would be an open and active dialogue between customer and supplier. This dialogue would transform a fairly vague set of requirements into the best specific set of time/cost/performance values available at the moment.

To achieve the necessary understanding between the customer and the supplier, the customer must include both those who are "buyers" and those who are "users," including those responsible for the installation, operation, and maintenance of the systems. The vendor must include those responsible for the design, manufacture, and service/repair of the systems. Through the involvement of all these, the process improvement team can identify the various required and desired characteristics that will form the basis of the trade-offs for the system process improvements.

In the ideal environment, the needs of the customer would be translated into increasingly more specific characteristics and features of the product. These, in turn, would be related directly to the process operations and capabilities that affect those specific product features. In this way, the "voice of the customer" would remain consistent and be heard by all those defining the product and process, and at all stages of the design process. To accomplish this, there must be both feed-forward and feed-back of information among various functional organizations (for example, the product-design team, the manufacturing-engineering team, and the production-planning team, etc.) and feed-forward between the various time phases of the product design process.

Similarly, there must exist a process whereby the customer and vendor can verify that the product, process, and support processes meet the requirements. Like the transmission and translation of these requirements just described, this must first occur at a "macro" level with evaluations that incorporate a significant degree of estimation and uncertainly. As the product and processes become further defined, the level of certainty and exactness of this verification will increase.

Requirements should be translated concurrently and in an integrated fashion into optimal product definitions, manufacturing processes, and support processes. Here, the key elements of improved operations relate to the simplification and integration of the creation of product and process definition, and the concurrent consideration of all phases of the product life cycle. The system simplification process must allow, encourage, and ensure that:

- All requirements of the system life cycle are considered and evaluated;

- The cross-impact of various functional decisions are understood and evaluated (with appropriate trade-off analysis);

- Critical risks of various design and manufacturing options are identified and addressed early in the process; and

- Those responsible for the various functional areas within the development and manufacturing enterprise participate with appropriate levels of responsibility and authority.

To achieve these integrated product and process development simplification objectives, four specific functions come to mind.[3]

First, there must be an integrated and continuing participation of multifunctional process improvement teams in the simplification of your products and processes. As the product designers improve your product concepts, others must simultaneously define the manufacturing process to achieve them. In a fully operational system for process design, the information system should have automatic access to the current capabilities and capacities of the corporate manufacturing facilities. This would permit you to project the impact of specific product tolerances and production volumes on the manufacturing system, and the adequacy of that system to meet your production requirements. Based on this knowledge, the designers of product and process can project costs at various levels of product/process performance, allowing informed decisions regarding the trade-offs of cost, quality, performance, and timing.

Second, this process of integrating multiple engineering, manufacturing, and management functions must provide for efficient iteration and closure of product and process designs. Each iteration should again involve each of the relevant functional process improvement teams for review of the impact of the changes made. This may be done manually through a marked-up blue-line drawing revision process, digitally through a process of automatic "flag raising," which notifies affected functions, or even with computer-aided analysis that can project the impact of design changes on the adequacy and/or projected performance and cost of the various life cycle elements (product capability, manufacturing process, service, reliability, etc.).

Third, the system must identify conflicting requirements and support their resolution through an objective choice of process options based upon a comparison of trade-offs. Any one change can increase product performance, but also increase manufacturing cost and time to production, and simultaneously decrease reliability. It is critical that your approach identifies, records, and analyzes such conflicts and the resulting trade-offs.

Finally, the system process must incorporate an optimization of the product and process design. This optimization can be based on either empirical or analytical knowledge. Empirical knowledge can be derived from experts in the field who call upon their experience to project the impact of design alternatives. Also, empirical knowledge can be systematically derived from data collected and statistically analyzed from current products and processes that are in some ways similar to those being developed. Analysis of theoretical knowledge and scientific/engineering analysis can also be applied to the evaluation of alternatives. These objectives will be met only when their application is assured and achieved with speed and ease.

MAP YOUR PROCESSES

"Process mapping" is a tool promoted by General Electric as part
of their "workout," "best practice," and "process mapping" strategy to improve their performance significantly. The idea is to
describe in writing or flow diagrams every single step in your
process, no matter how small, to help you understand what is
really going on in your business. Some of General Electric's
process maps were so detailed they covered whole walls. The
process maps allowed the process improvement teams to gain
real understanding of their processes.

At the General Electric Louisville appliance facility, process
mapping showed that "while a fifth of the parts in any given
appliance model were unique, only 5 percent were expensive
enough to substantially affect inventory costs. General Electric
found that it could speed manufacturing and cut costs by keeping
ample stocks of the cheap components, while working out just-
in-time programs with suppliers to quickly deliver the others as
needed. The biggest gains came from controlling the sequence in
which parts were delivered from a plant's loading dock to its
assembly line."[4]

Process mapping (PMAP) is an excellent near-term tool that
you can use to understand your current processes, and eliminate
or simplify those requiring change.

PMAP WORK-FLOW PROCESS MAPPING

The fundamental concepts of PMAP (process mapping) are based
on the ideas of structured analysis, which have produced significant payoffs in diverse business applications. Such benefits include reductions in development costs, fewer system integration
failures, and uniformly better communication. The basic PMAP
work-flow modeling concepts are:

1. Understand a process or system by creating a model that graphically shows things (objects or information) and activities (performed by men or machines).

2. Distinguish what functions a system must perform from how the system is built to accomplish those functions. The distinction must be clearly evident in the model.

3. Structure the model as a hierarchy with major functions at the top and successive process levels revealing well-bounded details. Each model must be internally consistent.

4. Establish an informal review cycle to "proofread" the developing model and record all decisions in writing. This ensures that the model reflects the best efforts of a committed team.

For new systems, projects, or processes, PMAP may be used to specify the requirements and functions, and then to improve the process that meets the customers' requirements and performs the required functions. For existing processes, PMAP can be used to analyze the purposes the application serves and the functions it performs, and, in addition, to record the mechanisms by which these are done. In all cases, the result of applying PMAP is a model, that is, a written description of a system. A PMAP model consists of diagrams, text, and glossary, cross-referenced to each other. Either paper or computer graphic process diagrams are the major output of the PMAP model. A PMAP model is represented using a graphic language designed to:

- Expose detail gradually and in a controlled manner;

- Encourage conciseness and accuracy;

- Focus attention on module interfaces;

- Provide a powerful analysis and design vocabulary.

A PMAP model considers activities, information, and interface constraints simultaneously. However, in any one model, the emphasis will always be on one of these aspects. For example, a process model shows activities as boxes and uses arrows to represent data and interfaces. Thus a representation—whether it be current operations, functional specification, or design—always consists of an activity model, an information model, and a user interface model.

PMAP always begins with a functional model, a representation of *what* the problem is, carefully separated from the design of *how* the problem will be solved or implemented. This ensures that the problem is fully and clearly understood before the details of a process solution are decided. The important feature is that the model shows *how* the *what* is to be realized. PMAP provides a notation to express how a function in the model is carried out by a mechanism, including how a single mechanism can perform related functions at several different places in the functional model.

PMAP starts by representing the whole system as a single modular unit—a box with arrow interfaces, as shown in figure 5.2. Since the single box represents the system as a whole, the descriptive name written in the box must be general, rather abstract, and lacking in detail. The same is true of the interface arrows, since they also represent the complete set of external interfaces to the system as a whole.

The box that represents the system as a single module is then detailed on another diagram with several boxes connected by interface arrows, as shown in figure 5.3. These interconnections make the boxes represent major submodules of the parent module. Each succeeding sublevel reveals a complete set of submodules, each represented as a box whose boundaries are defined by the interface arrows. Each of these submodule boxes may be similarly decomposed to expose even more detail.

PMAP provides rules covering how to introduce gradually further detail during decomposition. The upper limit of six boxes forces the use of a hierarchy to describe complex subjects. The

Figure 5.2   PMAP Top-Level Graphic Diagram

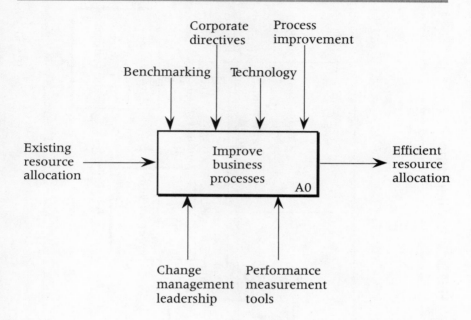

lower limit of three is usually chosen to ensure that enough detail is introduced to make the decomposition of interest.

Each diagram in a PMAP is shown in precise relationship to other diagrams by means of interconnecting arrows. When a module is decomposed into submodules, the interfaces between the submodules are shown as arrows. The name of each submodule box plus its labeled interfaces defines a context for the detailing of that submodule.

In all cases, every submodule is restricted to contain only those elements that lie within the scope of its parent module. Further, the module cannot omit any elements. The parent box and its interfaces provide a context. Nothing may be added or removed from this precise boundary.

The creation of a PMAP is carried out by process "authors." It is a dynamic process that usually requires the participation of more than one person; team action is preferred. Throughout a project,

Figure 5.3 PMAP Second Level Flow Diagram

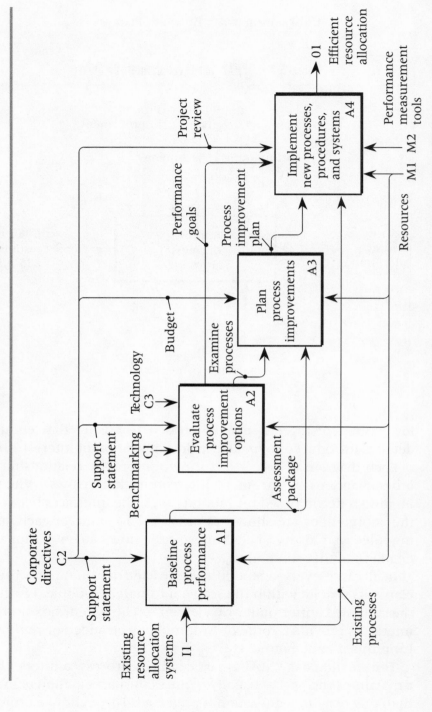

the draft versions of the diagrams produced are distributed to one or more other project members for review and comment. The discipline requires each person to make comments about a diagram, and then to submit them in writing to the "author" of the diagram. This cycle continues until the diagrams, and, eventually, the entire model are officially accepted. During the process, incorrect or unacceptable analysis and design results are usually spotted early, and oversights and errors are detected before they can cause major disruptions.

The end effect of this approach to organized process understanding and process improvement is a high assurance that the final PMAP models are valid. The diagrams are changed to reflect corrections and valid comments. More detail is added by the creation of more diagrams. More comments are made. More changes are included. The final model represents the agreement of the creators on a representation of the system or process being modeled.

PMAP AND SIMULATION

A process simulation is a model that changes over time. Generally, simulation addresses the dynamic properties that are often of greatest interest to process improvement. Simulation provides a relatively low-cost means to examine process improvements before substantial funds are invested in a new product or process improvement effort. Simulation of your processes are important for three specific reasons:

1. Process simulation provides a means of measuring overall changes in the value (output) of an organization or system caused by specific changes in your processes.

2. Process simulation's graphic capabilities help decision makers understand complex operations through a relatively simple graphic representation.

3. Process simulation identifies utilization rates of (money, time, people) activities, revealing bottlenecks or underutilized

activities. Bottlenecks tell you where to apply resources or suggest a redesign of your systems. Underutilized activities tell you where waste exists and identify resources for reallocation and activities that can be discontinued for a cost savings without degrading overall productivity.

Simulation also supports functional economic analysis in that it increases the possible dimensions of your cost/benefit analysis.

Proponents of any version of sophisticated structured process analysis tell us that activity models first require the establishment of purpose, context, and viewpoint. A complete viewpoint may be difficult, if not impossible, to establish using only PMAP descriptions. Simulation provides a suitable means of addressing this difficulty. Given that the functions represented by an activity model perform dynamically, three structural cases in an activity model imply a need to simulate process interaction changes.

When a process is structured so that an output from one activity provides input to two or more activities, organizational processes may "jam" because sequencing requirements are not met. Activity modeling will not reveal this deficiency, but simulation will. Effective process sequencing of activities can have a dramatic impact on the overall effectiveness of your business processes.

Also, when a process is structured so that an input to two or more activities comes from only one activity, organizational processes may "jam" over resource conflict, particularly consumable resources. If different activities are placing demands on a common pool of resources and the balance of those resources reaches zero, one or more activities will stall until the resources are resupplied. The process-wide impact of this effect can be marginal or substantial. Only through simulation can these impacts be quantified.

Finally, when outputs of two or more activities are inputs to each other, then parallelism (also known as concurrency) occurs.

This structural phenomenon represents coordination. Coordination is a prerequisite for process success when activities must exchange information or other resources with other activities at the same time. The efficiency of information exchange between concurrent or parallel activities can have counterintuitive, yet profound, effects on the length of time necessary to produce a product or process.

Simulation addresses aspects of processes for which activity and data modeling are inadequately suited. Since activity and data models are static, they cannot cope with the impact of resource flow. Simulation is an excellent method for this purpose and, as a result, can provide insight that may be a more truthful representation of reality. In the context of other process improvement methodologies, there are two general areas to which simulation may contribute uniquely. These are in dynamically measuring activity utilization and system workload.

Activity Utilization

In a steady-state environment, activity utilization can be measured using static techniques. Activity-based costing is an accounting technique that involves measuring both the cost and value of activities. It may be possible to identify the resources supporting each activity and their sunk costs in dynamic processes, but difficult, however, to measure the proportion of these resources actually devoted to one activity. Simulation can provide these measures. Simulation demonstrates bottlenecks and underutilization of activities or equipment, enabling management to redistribute resources or restructure processes to enhance overall efficiency.

System Workload

Another capability simulation provides to process improvement is in linking local changes to global measures. One aspect of activity modeling is the development of a "to-be" model. The options for projecting a "to-be" model can be unlimited. Many different collections of relationships can be redefined between activities, and the application of resources used by activities can be varied in many different ways. When two or more "to-be" models are under consideration, how does one choose the best alternative? Simulation provides a means of measuring anticipated global performance when changes are made locally.

WORK-FLOW PROCESS SIMULATION TOOLS

Work-flow process simulation tools are of two general types:

Discrete event simulations show processes as a sequence of events in which each event has a beginning and an ending point, usually measured by time. Consequently, discrete event simulations are often called time-step simulations. Associated with these discrete points in time are state variables that measure the state of the process being simulated. Therefore, as a simulation proceeds through a series of events, the process under simulation will be viewed as a series of state changes. Analysis can focus either globally or locally as designed in any particular simulation.

Continuous event simulations show processes with mathematical expressions that do not delineate discrete events. The process analyst can designate a sequence of points in time to provide a sequence of snapshots of the simulated process.

There are advantages and disadvantages to either type of simulation. Discrete event simulations generally provide a better format for analysis in that it may be easier to structure a process simulation through the building-block approach provided by them. Discrete events facilitate postsimulation analysis, keyed to the initiation and completion of events. The downside of discrete event simulation includes the increased labor required to construct a simulation at a discrete event level and the demands on computational capability required. Some discrete event simulations will be infeasible because of the number of events that must be considered.

Continuous event simulations are easier to use after a choice has been made of the mathematical expressions used to construct them. They generally require less time and labor in setup and in postsimulation analysis. They can also demand less computer power. For these reasons, they support more computer runs, allowing wider variance in cases that can be considered. Their weak point is in how well the mathematical expressions fit the processes being simulated. Although some expressions provide excellent representations of simulated processes, others may include unacceptable errors or unknown side effects.

Several current simulation techniques are worthy of comment. Five techniques selected for comment here include Petri nets, ITHINK system dynamics, SIMSCRIPT, custom software, and flowchart graphic packages.

Petri nets are particularly useful in discrete simulation. IDEF/PMAP activity models can map into Petri net structures and are easy to construct and analyze, and can replicate phenomena difficult to model using other simulation techniques. Excellent Petri net tools include the Air Force–developed software MODELER and the commercially developed Meta Software Corporation (Cambridge, Massachusetts) work-flow analyzer called Design/CPN. MODELER has an edge over Design/CPN in that it is more object oriented, has a better user interface, and costs less. Meta Software is working to provide a PC-based system at a lower cost. Design/CPN has been designed for integration with activity models using an automatic programming feature and is more flexible in the range of simulations to which it can be applied. The integration feature of Design/CPN and MODELER is so strong that they each could accurately be described as CASE tools that semiautomatically convert information requirements into computer code. Design/CPN can be an effective tool not only to map your processes, it can also be used as a graphical report-writing product that can document your processes for ISO 9000 certification.

ITHINK is a powerful system dynamics continuous-type tool for the study of resource allocation. ITHINK is a commercially developed software program that currently costs less than

Design/CPN, and does not require a lot of expertise to apply. Weak characteristics are that it does not accommodate hierarchy and would be difficult to integrate with some activity models and/or data models.

Custom software is not generally recommended for use because of the high cost required to develop it.

There are several new products that are oriented toward use of personal computers and Windows™ software for process mapping (PMAP) based on the U.S. Air Force IDEF model. They include Logic Works Inc. (1060 Route 206, Princeton, New Jersey 08540, 609-252-1177) BP*win* and ER*win*. BP*win* is a powerful, fast, and easy to use Windows-based business processing re-engineering tool that is designed to help you define and optimize your business processes. It provides the IDEF0 Business Processing modeling linked to ER*win* for IDEF1X Data Modeling and Database generation, that can be linked to a variety of target server databases. Another IDEF based product is by Wizdom Systems, Inc. (1300 Iroquois Avenue, Naperville, Illinois 60563, 708-357-3000). Their approach provides a series of tools, such as Wizdom Works, IDEFine, IDEFine-0, IDEFine-1X, IDEFglossary, IDEFcost, IDEFast, IDEFlow, IDEFqual, IDEFplan, and IDEFbpi, which is their trademarks. Wizdom Systems works with the CACI International (703-841-4430) Simulation Software.

There are also Windows flowchart graphic drawing tools such as a product called Optima, that is developed by AdvanEdge Technologies, Inc., (503-692-8162) in Tualatin, Oregon. Optima provides a simple-to-use, inexpensive product to start your process analysis.

In summary, PMAP provides a disciplined way of describing the detailed structure of your processes and how they relate to each other. Since understanding hierarchy is important in understanding large, complex systems, PMAP (based on IDEF) is particularly useful, since it includes hierarchy as an element of its modeling capability. PMAP can help define the structure that exists between processes for effective simulation, analysis, and process improvement.

CHAPTER 6

Don't Do It Again and Again

CUT YOUR REWORK

Rework is killing the productivity and competitiveness of many large and small businesses in America. The rework (the lost effort in doing over and over again an activity that was flawed) rate for administrative and information-based activities can run as high as 40 to 60 percent, while rework rates in product manufacturing can run 20 to 40 percent.

Many of the survival-based cost-cutting activities are focused on significantly reducing rework. These efforts usually are addressed by implementing total quality management "bottom-up" continuous process improvement techniques to significantly reduce your rework. For example, in many Japanese manufacturing operations, their rework rate is in the 3 to 5 percent range, due in part to their concentration on wide-scale adoption of total quality management practices. This chapter provides an overview of total quality management, and a seventeen-step planning and implementation process that you can tailor to your business.[1]

Total quality management means that you are meeting your internal and external customers' requirements by doing "the right things right the first time." To provide high-quality products and services, management must believe that an obsession for quality and near-perfection must pervade every facet of your business. The driving force behind total quality management is customer satisfaction.

Total quality management begins with a strategic decision, a decision that must be made and fully supported by top management. That decision, simply put, is the decision to survive by competing as a quality-driven business. Total quality management concentrates on improving your performance as the primary strategy to achieve your near-term goals. It requires that you take a systematic view of your business, at how each business unit, function, and process contributes to your survival.

The total quality management methodology is based on four concepts. These concepts state that: (1) your business must have a management-driven total quality management system; (2) it must insist on quality products, services, and technology; (3) it must employ quality people; (4) and that the combined energies of your management team must be focused on customer satisfaction.

Total quality management provides a point of departure framework for your application of its concepts, principles, and practices in terms of your specific near-term needs.

WHAT IS TOTAL QUALITY MANAGEMENT?

Total quality management is not a minor refinement of past managerial practices. What sets total quality management apart from other approaches to management is a genuinely new perspective of how to best combine or reengineer the resources (people, budget, programs) that change your business to obtain breakthrough performance gains to help you survive. Total quality management involves a unique set of organizing principles, a new role for top management and co-workers alike, and an array of practices and techniques designed to implement these organizing principles. In other words, total quality management is both a comprehensive managerial philosophy and a tool kit for its implementation.

Some managers feel total quality management is a radical departure from traditional management practices due to its analytic focus on work-flow processes and statistical process control rather than function or product. Others question its insistence that the customer is best equipped to define the quality of your work.

Still other critics worry about the new roles assigned to the "empowered" co-worker in a total quality management organization. Since workers and processes are the basic sources from which quality flows, every co-worker in a total quality management organization, from president to custodian, and every process, from the handling of invoices to processing customer complaints, has one central and common purpose: to improve the quality of the organization's services and products to help satisfy the customer.

In a total quality management context, the standard for determining quality is meeting customer requirements and expectations the first time and every time. There are many potential requirements and expectations that customers have, depending upon the particular product or service and needs of the customer. Rather than the organization attempting to specify what it views as quality, a total quality management approach systematically inquires of its customers what they want, and strives to meet, and even exceed, those requirements. Such an approach helps to identify the elements of quality that are of paramount importance to your customers. It also recognizes that customers' expectations may change over time.

Total Quality Management is a strategic, integrated management system for achieving customer satisfaction. It involves all managers and employees and uses quantitative methods to improve continuously an organization's processes. It is not an efficiency ("cost-cutting") program, a morale-boosting scheme, a downsizing (rightsizing) program, or a project that can be delegated to operational managers and staff specialists. Paying lip service to quality improvements by merely using quality slogans to exhort workers is equally dangerous.

At the foundation of total quality management (see figure 6.1) are three principles: (1) focus on achieving customer satisfaction; (2) seek continuous improvement; and (3) give everyone responsibility.

The basic total quality management message sent to managers is this: to remain responsive to changing customer demands, the organization itself must be ready and able to both detect the need for change *and* to maintain the ability to make the needed changes to continue to satisfy the customer.

Figure 6.1   Total Quality Management Principles

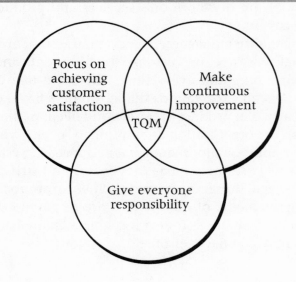

For total quality management, we define "quality" as the extent to which services and products produced conform to customer requirements. Customers can be internal as well as external to the organizational system (e.g., products or services may flow to the person at the next desk or work area rather than to people outside the immediate organization).

The days of limiting the definition of quality to the "soundness" of the product—its hardness or durability, for example—are gone. The new kind of quality America rediscovered in the 1990s is far more cultural than physical, far more the way things are done than the nature of the things themselves.

TOTAL QUALITY MANAGEMENT OPERATING PRACTICES

To define total quality management is one thing. To implement it is another. As we shall see, total quality management is far more than tinkering with an organization's structure.

Shifting from a traditional, functional view of an organization to one based on work-flow processes is not an easy task, but near-term success has been demonstrated.

Businesses that have adopted total quality management (1) focus on *achieving customer satisfaction,* (2) seek *continuous and long-term improvement* in all of the organization's processes and outputs, and (3) take steps to assure the *full involvement of the entire workforce in improving quality*. These are the three principles of total quality management to maximize customer satisfaction.

The essence of total quality management is involving and empowering your employees to improve the quality of goods and services continuously in order to satisfy, and even delight, your customers. To achieve this goal requires identifying customers and their needs, having a clear idea of how the organization plans to go about meeting expectations, and making sure that everyone in the organization understands the customers' needs and is empowered to act on their behalf.

How does an organization achieve a commitment to total quality management that meets the above description? Business survivors emphasize several total quality management practices, summarized below, which, when integrated as part of your strategy, result in the fundamental near-term changes required.

Top Management Leadership

The primary, and perhaps the most critical, single element in the total quality management equation is the role of top management leadership and support. Top management leaders must be directly and actively involved in establishing a new environment that encourages change, innovation, risk taking, pride in work, and continuous improvement on behalf of all your customers. These top-level leaders set the tone, determine the theme, and provide impetus for action throughout the organization. They assert a clear vision of what the organization can achieve, and they communicate the quality policies and goals throughout the organization. This means providing an active, visible presence to all members of the workforce, and the required resources, time, and training essential to improve your quality.

All employees, including union leadership, in the early stages of the quality planning process, must be an integral part of the transition to total quality management. The total quality management leader will empower workers on the line to make decisions. Leaders will shift their efforts from directing and controlling how the operations will be carried out to identifying and removing barriers that prevent employees from meeting customer requirements and expectations. They lead the fundamental cultural change in the organization from crisis management to continuous improvement.

In a total quality management organization, worker "empowerment" means that the supervisory and control responsibilities that are commonly reserved for senior managers in traditional organizations are entrusted to cross-functional teams of workers that, on a day-to-day basis, transform inputs into outputs. Top leaders "empower" workers by giving each process team the freedom to set goals, and the tools to achieve them. Ideally, the inspection function can be reduced in a total quality management organization because each worker is committed to doing his or her job "right the first time."

Strategic Planning

Strategic survival planning drives your business's improvement efforts. Planning for quality improvement is integrated into the strategic planning process, so that planning and achieving quality improvement become a part of the day-to-day management of the operation. Further, establishing a dynamic, participative planning *process* is as important as developing the plan itself.

A critical objective of total quality management is to develop a climate or culture in your business that encourages pursuit of excellence on behalf of customers and that nurtures risk taking and employee participation. A primary goal of the strategic plan is to map out the near-term strategy to bring about the cultural change. The plan establishes the goals for attaining superior levels of customer satisfaction and organizational performance. Thus, it both looks outward to the customer and focuses inward on the organization's processes. The plan, which is updated periodically, defines how the organization intends to fulfill customer expectations over the next year or two.

Everyone in the organization should contribute ideas to the plan and be aware of its implications for his or her own areas of responsibility. In organizations where employees are represented by unions, management should enlist the support and participation of union officials. Both management and organized labor benefit from the active involvement of labor in planning and carrying out the quality improvement processes.

Focus on the Customer

World-class organizations seek not only to meet customer expectations, but also to go the extra mile and delight both their internal and external customers. Actively involving customers in the improvement process and finding out exactly what they want is central to a total quality management effort.

The concept of customer focus applies to both internal and external customers. Within an organization, work normally is organized so that the product of one worker is passed on to another before a final product or service is delivered. Under a total quality management approach, any worker who delivers a product or service to someone else sees that person as a customer and attempts to determine his or her needs and requirements in order to improve the quality of the final product or service.

Depending on its special needs, each business should have a wide range of methods for obtaining and assessing customer feedback, including: customer surveys, in-depth interviews of groups of customers, follow-up of customer complaints, collection of customer feedback at the time of service delivery, and third-party analysis of customer feedback. Customers should have easy access to the organization for obtaining information and resolution of their problems. Quality organizations adopt a service orientation as the primary means of achieving their mission.

Teamwork and Employee Empowerment

Once top management has made the long-term commitment to total quality management, the most important and critical ingredient to achieving a quality commitment throughout an organization is employee involvement, empowerment, and teamwork. Improving work processes can be successful only when all people in the organization, top to bottom and horizontally across functions, are involved in making the changes. When the intelligence, imagination, and energies of the entire workforce are engaged in the pursuit of the organization's goals, lasting results can be realized. People closest to the problems usually have the best information sources and solutions.

The idea of employee involvement, participative management, and empowerment is not unique to total quality management. Indeed, many management practitioners claim to support the idea. Efforts often fall short, not because of the absence of good intentions on the part of managers or co-workers, but because managers have not adopted specific systems and procedures to make employee involvement a routine part of the new way of providing better service to your customers.

The first step in achieving employee empowerment is to involve employees systematically in identifying and solving problems, including teams of employees working on specific process or operating issues, cross-functional problem-solving teams, and self-managing teams. The key is that employees be empowered to make real and lasting changes.

One of the most powerful employee involvement techniques is to engage teams of workers (often called quality improvement teams or process action teams) in addressing immediate operational issues that the team itself helps identify and resolve. When line workers participate in identifying and solving problems that are affecting the quality of the work they perform, they experience the satisfaction of making tangible contributions to the quality of their work and frequently are motivated to make continuing and lasting improvements to the work they do. Obviously, these results will not occur without the active support and responsiveness of management.

Employee involvement in quality improvement teams must be supported and reinforced by building into the organization's management system explicit recognition and support for the team concept. Management should focus on establishing and taking responsibility for approving employee teams at the outset, assigning resources to let the teams perform their mission, and, perhaps most importantly, authorizing changes in overall systems and policies necessary to implement the solutions.

The employee involvement strategy should include organized labor at all stages in the process so that union leaders understand what is planned and can support the effort. Managers must be prepared to listen and where possible adopt recommendations of workers, delegating greater responsibility to lower levels in the organization. If they do, everyone will feel "ownership" of quality improvement and will exhibit personal pride in the quality of their work.

Employees are an almost unlimited source of knowledge and creativity that can be used, not only to solve problems, but also to improve continuously the quality of the services and products they produce.

Continuous Process Improvement

One of total quality management's overall implementing methodologies is continuous process improvement. Each process team is constantly trying to improve the performance of their work process—from input from their supplier to output to their customers.

Statistical control methods are used to reduce rework, waste, and cycle time, and to measure the extent to which your business is satisfying your customers' demands.

Commitment to Training and Recognition

Often the key element that is missing in efforts to improve workflow processes is the training that will enable empowered teams of co-workers to do their job. This includes adequate training in classrooms and on the job to ensure that employees are equipped with the skills to perform their work. It also includes training in quality management concepts and skills such as teamwork, problem-solving skills, team communication, and methods for collecting and analyzing data using basic statistical tools.

Co-workers who make contributions to quality improvement should be recognized and rewarded in ways that are meaningful and timely. Reinforcing positive performance is a key ingredient for developing service excellence. An organization that only claims to be focused on quality, but, in fact, measures and rewards other things, sends conflicting messages to its employees.

Nonmonetary awards and recognition can have a powerful and lasting impact on employee motivation and commitment. The experience of many organizations facing stringent budget constraints and rigid compensation systems is that creative recognition systems can go a long way toward achieving co-worker participation in service improvement.

Measurement and Analysis

Many managers depend on intuition and seat-of-the-pants judgments to solve problems. In a total quality management organization, however, as many decisions as possible must be based on hard data.

Statistical process control systems are crucial, and must be put in place to allow each work process improvement team in the organization to systematically measure the degree to which it is achieving its quality goals and the degree to which its output satisfies their customers' expectations. Seat-of-the-pants judgment is best replaced with objective data.

Data should be collected on a wide selection of customer satisfaction factors, such as responsiveness, reliability, accuracy, and so forth. Measurement systems should also focus on internal processes, especially on key processes that generate variation in quality and cycle time.

TOTAL QUALITY MANAGEMENT IS UNIQUE

Although the adoption and integration of the total quality management operating practices are very important, managers beginning a total quality management effort should bear in mind that to realize the full potential of total quality management requires a fundamental cultural change. When this transformation has occurred, everyone in the organization is continuously and systematically working to improve the quality of services and goods, and the processes for delivering them, in order to maximize customer satisfaction. Total quality management becomes a way of managing that is embedded in the culture and environment of the organization, not simply a set of specific management techniques and tools.

A total quality management approach to management represents a unique blending of: (1) the objective, practical, and quantitative aspects of management, e.g., focus on processes and reliance on quantitative data and statistical analysis for decision making; and (2) the "soft" aspects of management, e.g., providing visionary leadership, promoting a spirit of cooperation and teamwork, and practicing participative management. Many businesses when deciding to undertake a total quality management effort focus on one or the other of these general approaches. A fully successful effort requires balanced attention to both.

Although many of the principles and operating practices summarized above are familiar, and many managers believe they already practice them, *many aspects of total quality management are in fact unique*. For instance:

- Many organizations claim to serve the customer first, but few systematically and rigorously identify the needs of customers, both internal and external, and monitor the extent to which those needs are being met.

- Many managers encourage employee involvement and empowerment, but few organizations adopt the specific practices that bring them about, such as reliance on teams of employees to identify and resolve specific operating problems. When teams are used, few have been delegated sufficient authority to make changes or have been trained to use the proper set of total quality management tools.

❏ Although many organizations recognize the importance of measurement and analysis to decision making, many measure the wrong things. Also, few organizations focus on internal processes across functions in order to assure that quality is built into the production and service system on a continuing basis.

❏ Many organizations have in place a system they call "quality assurance," but these systems are often designed to check for adherence to quality standards at the end of the production process. Total quality management creates procedures for assuring quality throughout the production and service process.

Where total quality management has been adopted by organizations, the results have been startling. Workers at all levels focus on their customers' needs and become committed and involved in the quest for quality. Management and co-workers form a team in seeking continuous improvement. The cumulative result of these changes frequently is a significant change in the overall culture and atmosphere of the organization. Organizations become more streamlined, a larger percentage of workers are involved in line operations, and there is a greater spirit of cooperation and working toward common goals. Perhaps most significantly, a spirit of energy and excitement can permeate your business survival activities.

THE COST OF QUALITY

One of the more compelling reasons prompting business survivors (such as Xerox, Motorola, and Harley-Davidson) to trade in traditional management practices for total quality management practices was the projected cost of poor quality if they continued to do business as usual. Once managers realized how costly their old way of doing business was—mainly because it actually built poor quality and unnecessary rework costs into the process—shifting to a new, defect-free process became very attractive financially. According to *A Guide for Implementing Total Quality Management*, from the Reliability Analysis Center, the "cost of poor quality has been quoted by various sources as being between 15% to 50% of the cost of operations. . . . One of the most effective actions management can take to improve productivity in any organization is to improve the quality of its processes. Quality saves, it does not cost. . . . Reducing the cost of poor quality directly affects your budget."[2]

The key event, then, in an organization's journey toward total quality management is an awareness among top management that their budgets already reflect the costs of not doing things right the first time around. They must change their definition of quality, and, to assure their survival, the total quality management program should be implemented organization-wide and involve everyone at all levels.

Simply stated, the cost of quality aims at using your budget wisely and avoiding waste. At Xerox, the "Cost of Quality is defined as the measurement of what your division, department, teamwork group or family group is spending for its overall quality."[3] There are three kinds of measurements in cost of quality:

Cost to Conform

Spending that is in conformance with customer requirements. Conformance means that work outputs are being measured against known customer requirements.

Cost of Nonconformance

Spending that is not in conformance with customer requirements, and is measured in the time and cost needed to go back and do a job over.

Lost Opportunities

When a customer is lost due to your poor quality and value.

Figure 6.2 will help you visualize the cost shifts that can be expected as your organization adopts quality management.

Implicit in this cost of quality diagram is the notion that your business should continuously set, and achieve, higher quality standards. Also, the return on quality investment should pay off.

TOTAL QUALITY MANAGEMENT DO'S AND DON'TS

The following do's and don'ts are a compilation of lessons learned in successful business organizations that can help guide you in your total quality management improvement efforts:

Do's

- ❑ Do capitalize on previous experience and lessons learned.

- ❑ Do keep survival strategy and business mission, rather than turf battles, in forefront.

Figure 6.2   The Cost of Quality: Before and After Total Quality Management

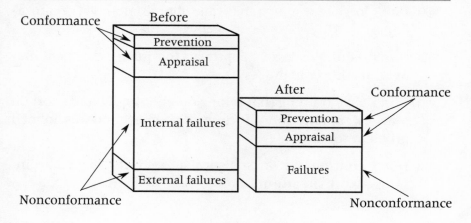

❑ Do see yourself as a leader of change.

❑ Do keep the message simple and uncomplicated.

❑ Do make use of every possible communication opportunity to reinforce quality.

❑ Do concentrate on attitude instead of tools and techniques in the beginning.

❑ Do it, don't study it to death.

❑ Do support champions by using early project teams.

❑ Do involve middle managers early on.

❑ Do tailor training to fit your unique business needs.

❑ Do include input from your customers in setting your course of direction and in prioritizing activities.

❑ Do involve unions from the beginning of the process.

. . . and Don'ts

❑ Don't call it total quality management if you don't want to, but do total quality management.

❑ Don't plan so carefully that you never get started.

❑ Don't force one approach on all subordinate-level organizations.

❑ Don't require excessive approvals for quality change initiatives; it stifles the process.

❑ Don't have training that is long on philosophy and short on practical application of concepts, tools, and disciplined problem solving.

❑ Don't concentrate on statistical procedures in the beginning—work on attitudes.

THE TRANSITION TO TOTAL
QUALITY MANAGEMENT

Earlier in this chapter, we discussed the coming shift from traditional management to total quality management practices. Once this shift takes place, total quality management practices will displace existing practices—that is, they will become standard operating procedures. Until that paradigm shift takes place, however, the process of introducing and institutionalizing a set of new management ideas in an existing organization will be a difficult task.

Each new procedure introduced into an organization is certain to upset an existing status quo. Workers who identify personally with the existing status quo will, in turn, feel vulnerable and insecure. Their response is likely to be resistance to the new ideas and the changes in behavior required to implement them. For this reason, if a new idea is to pass from simply being a new concept to actual practice in an organization, it needs continued support from your quality champions.

A quality champion is needed to overcome the resistance the change process will generate and to settle the myriad of problems and barriers that will crop up from day to day. In the absence of a dedicated champion, the initiation of a new idea will soon falter before it is routinized. A total quality management champion, an individual who leads by his or her own participation, is needed to inspire others to enter fully into the change process. A successful total quality management champion will:

- Visibly support the organization's total quality management strategy.

- Insist on the team approach.

- Measure his or her success by customer satisfaction.

❑ Build feedback loops within the firm and to suppliers and customers.

❑ Meet performance, profitability, and return on quality goals.

The question now is, Does your organization have a total quality management champion? If not, why not you?

IMPROVE YOUR QUALITY NOW!

This chapter has described the need for you to implement a total quality management methodology. By tailoring these total quality management concepts and principles to your unique business, you can significantly improve your quality, increase productivity, provide better service to your customers, and help assure your business survival.

Business organizations all too often have jumped to implement new "hot" buzzword solutions to their problems. We tend to spend too little time, thought, and energy on development of the organization's policy and planning needs to implement your near-term actions. The Japanese, for example, spend half of their effort on consensus building, developing understanding of their customer needs, and reviewing options for implementation. Then they think through all the steps needed to implement this change or process. In America, we tend to spend less than one-third of our efforts on planning, then jump into the implementation phase and continue to "fight fires" to resolve the errors and inconsistencies that with proper planning we could have avoided. The concept of "doing things right the first time" depends on realistic, thorough planning and management leadership.

To assist you in developing your plan, a total of seventeen planning and implementation steps has been delineated below for your review, modification, and adoption in your own unique total quality management program.

A PLAN FOR ACTION

The ten planning steps (see figure 6.3) needed to help you identify your policy and plans for implementing a total quality management program in your business are described below:

Step 1. Top Management Commitment to Total Quality Management

Simply put, total quality management is a new way for organizations to do business. Since the methods by which an organization conducts its business are clearly the prerogative of top management, it is, therefore, top management that must be convinced of the merits of total quality management. Top management's recognition of the need for improvement and its willingness to learn more are the first steps toward implementation.

It is probably not possible to overstate the importance of the role of top management. Leadership is essential during every phase in the development of your organization's total quality management program, and is particularly vital at the initial stages of planning. In fact, indifference and lack of involvement by top management are frequently cited as the principal reasons for the failure of total quality management improvement efforts.

To be successfully implemented, total quality management requires not only the vision, planning, and active involved leadership of top management, it also requires such practical support as providing the resources for implementation—the necessary time, money, and personnel needed. Delegation and rhetoric are insufficient.

To obtain top management commitment, you need to begin to educate senior managers regarding the impact of how your business can be enhanced by total quality management. You need to encourage them to learn the basic philosophy, principles, and

Figure 6.3   Total Quality Management Planning Steps

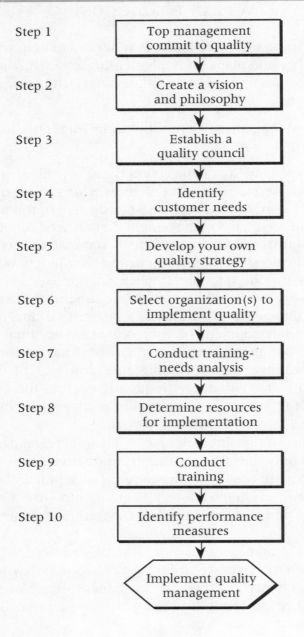

Step 1 — Top management commit to quality

Step 2 — Create a vision and philosophy

Step 3 — Establish a quality council

Step 4 — Identify customer needs

Step 5 — Develop your own quality strategy

Step 6 — Select organization(s) to implement quality

Step 7 — Conduct training-needs analysis

Step 8 — Determine resources for implementation

Step 9 — Conduct training

Step 10 — Identify performance measures

Implement quality management

practices involved in making your business policy one that focuses on total quality management.

The bottom line is that top management must enthusiastically participate in changing your organization's culture. Table 6.1 identifies some of the culture changes that your top management needs to understand and address to achieve improved quality. Without top management's active participation as the champions of total quality management, your organization will not obtain the full scope of benefits possible.

Step 2. Create a Vision and Philosophy

A key step in the total quality management process is the creation of a common understanding among top managers about what they want the organization to look like in the near-term and what principles will guide the actions they take to achieve the desired future. These agreements will become the basis for formal statements of the organization's vision and values.

The vision is a clear, positive, forceful statement of what the organization wants to be within two years. It is expressed in simple, specific terms. The vision allows the organization to stretch and aim for a higher goal. The vision must be powerful enough to excite people and show them the way things could be. A well-crafted vision statement supported by action can be a powerful tool for focusing your business toward a common goal.

Whatever form the vision and guiding principles take, it is important that they be communicated throughout your business frequently and with conviction. The timing and method of communication provide an opportunity for creativity by top management. It is important that the vision be followed soon by a concrete plan of action to avoid its being dismissed as a hollow slogan.

Table 6.1 Examples of Total Quality Management Cultural Change

CATEGORY	PREVIOUS STATE	NEW CULTURE
Mission	Maximum return on investment (ROI)/ management by objectives (MBO)	Ethical behavior and customer satisfaction; climate for continuous improvement; ROI a performance measure
Customer requirements	Incomplete or ambiguous understanding of customer requirements	Use of a systematic approach to seek out, understand, and satisfy both internal and external customer requirements
Suppliers	Unidirectional relationship	Partnership
Objectives	Orientation to short-term objectives and actions with limited long-term perspective	Deliberate balance of long-term goals with successive short-term objectives
Improvement	Acceptance of process variability and subsequent corrective action assigning blame as the norm	Understanding and improving the process
Problem solving	Unstructured individualistic problem solving and decision making	Predominantly participatory and interdisciplinary problem solving and decision making based on substantive data

CATEGORY	PREVIOUS STATE	NEW CULTURE
Jobs and people	Functional, narrow scope; management controlled	Management and employee involvement; work teams; integrated functions
Management style	Management style with uncertain objectives, which instills fear of failure	Open style with clear and consistent objectives, which encourages group-derived continuous improvement
Role of manager	Plan, organize, assign, control, and enforce	Communicate, consult, delegate, coach, mentor, remove barriers, and establish trust
Rewards and recognition	Pay by job; few team incentives	Individual and group recognition and rewards, negotiated criteria
Measurement	Orientation toward data gathering for problem identification	Data used to understand and continuously improve processes

Step 3. Establish Total Quality Management Council

Developing an organization structure that will institute, sustain, and facilitate expansion of your total quality management improvement effort is an essential element for success. The structure is the vehicle for focusing the energy and resources of the organization toward one common goal—continuous improvement of the products and services it provides to your customers.

Successful business organizations tailor the structure so that it maximizes strong points and accommodates their unique mission, culture, and approach for improving quality. This accounts for some of the differences in the way organizational charts are drawn and for variations in the nomenclature used to describe the total quality management organization. In spite of these differences, several common practices emerge that merit examination.

Virtually every organization that has successfully introduced the total quality management approach has formed a Quality Council of top managers during the early stages of implementation. This team is also sometimes called the Executive Steering Committee (ESC) or Executive Steering Group (ESG) or Executive Quality Council (EQC).

By establishing your Quality Council, top management provides identity, structure, and legitimacy to the total quality management improvement effort. It is the first concrete indication that top management has recognized the need to improve and has begun to change the way the organization conducts business. The direction this change will take becomes clear when the Quality Council publishes its vision, guiding principles, and mission statement.

The Quality Council is chaired by a very senior executive and includes membership of the senior management team. The Quality Council is responsible for launching, coordinating, and overseeing the total quality management improvement effort.

Quality Councils also can be used to link your total quality management organization together. Vertical linkage is accomplished by having a member of a top-level Quality Council serve as chairperson of a lower-level (second tier) council. A member of that council, in turn, chairs a lower-level (third tier) council or leads a subordinate-level team. Horizontal linkage is accomplished by having members of different functional departments (e.g., personnel, administration, service, finance) serve together on cross-functional teams.

This total quality management council structural linkage offers a number of benefits to your organization.

- It helps the organization stay focused on pursuing the same goals rather than have functional departments working at cross-purposes.

- It fosters better teamwork and less internal competition.

- It improves communication throughout the organization and better understanding of how all the pieces fit together.

- It improves the ability to replicate ideas and standardize solutions that have applicability to processes in other departments of the organization.

Step 4. Identify Customer Needs

Quality means that your organization is meeting your customers' expectations. Customers can be co-workers (internal customers) or end users (external customers) of your services or products.

Expectations are your customers' needs and wants. Meeting customer expectations through application of total quality management principles is the key to your productive future.

Use of the customer/supplier/co-worker model is an excellent technique for determining what your customers want, need, or expect. Only by interaction between the supplier (you) and the customer can this be answered.

The customer/supplier model was designed to analyze and help improve your customer needs analysis. It involves four key steps:

- Define your process or task.

- Define your value-added contribution to that process.

- Define your customer's expectations—i.e., negotiate specific "requirements" and define appropriate feedback of measurements.

- Communicate with your supplier and negotiate your requirements and feedback mechanisms just as you did with your customer.

To define "requirements" and "feedback" consider:

- Requirements are the most critical key characteristics of your output as defined by your customer.

- Feedback from your customer communicates the degree to which your output conforms to the requirements negotiated with your customer.

Taking these simple steps will significantly improve the quality of your work as it is defined by the most important person in the process: your customer.

Step 5. Develop Your Own Unique Strategy

There is no *one* right way to implement total quality management successfully in your business, no guaranteed recipe for success. The process proposed in this book is a synthesis of approaches used successfully by businesses that have survived. It is offered only as a guide in developing strategies and associated plans to carry out these strategies. The intent of a flexible approach is to capitalize on your business's strong points to allow energy to be focused on key improvement opportunities.

Furthermore, it would be useless to graft the experience of one business organization wholesale onto another, without tailoring it to meet the unique needs of that second organization.

The best plans are those that result in action—action that improves the processes of the business and results in better services and products for the customer. A simple plan that generates action and gets results is better than an elaborate plan that collects dust. Some initial total quality management strategic actions might consist of specific projects designed to address system-wide problems that have potential for expanding to other processes of the organization; or there might be efforts to implement total quality management in one organization or across the board. Examples of such efforts might include:

❏ Create a team to review the total quality management concept and define unique strategy for your organization.

❏ Conduct customer surveys and communicate benchmark results that should be used as quality indicators.

❏ Create quality teams to address specific known operating problems.

❏ Define your own unique total quality management problem-solving process.

❏ Define your own total quality management improvement plan.

It is a good idea for your organization to have at least begun in some key areas the process of identifying customers, their requirements, and reviewing quality indicators for services or products. This might occur in organizational components in which total quality management will be implemented initially, or on a more widescale basis in anticipation of future total quality management implementation.

Step 6. Select Organization(s) to Implement Total Quality Management

At the outset of your quality improvement effort, organizations usually choose to implement total quality management either organization-wide or with one or more pilots. It is also possible to tailor a combination of the two approaches to fit particular circumstances. In any case, the decision is one that each organization must make after realistically assessing a number of factors, including:

❑ The size and complexity of the organization.

❑ The ability of the organization to change.

❑ The resources (time and money and people) that can be allocated to introduce and sustain the effort.

❑ The level and intensity of support for total quality management throughout the organization.

Implementing total quality management on a broad scale across a large organization is a major undertaking. It requires significant allocations of time, money, and people, and for most organizations requires substantive operational and cultural changes. The larger the organization, the more massive the change.

Some advantages to broadscale implementation are as follows:

❑ It promotes consistent implementation. Each organizational element uses the same total quality management philosophy, language, and training, and is guided by the same vision and core principles.

❑ The decision to implement organization-wide demonstrates strong commitment at the very top level of the organization. This can facilitate the removal of barriers between organizations.

❑ The total quality management organization structure can be cascaded throughout a company, providing linkage between the corporate headquarters and operating units for improved communications.

❑ It provides for economies of scale (procuring consultant services, for example, or developing in-house training support). For instance, a large training contract is generally less expensive per person than a series of smaller contracts.

❑ It allows the organization to capitalize on its staff offices to support implementation. For example, statistical specialists located at the organization management level can be used to provide technical assistance to operating units.

You are encouraged to study closely your peers' efforts before undertaking a similar venture.

Some organizations have found advantages to starting pilot efforts rather than total organization adoption, including:

❑ Initial expenditures of resources are less.

❑ Development of wholly new services allows organization to start from "greenfield" and create new quality culture from the start.

❑ Resistance to change is minimized by targeting locations where local "champions" reside. Alternatively, the effort can be planned for success by targeting locations that have demonstrated adaptability to change by participating successfully in previous pilot efforts.

❑ Early successes can be used to galvanize support in other parts of the organization. Skeptics can be converted by seeing that it can work in their company.

❑ Early failures can be turned into lessons learned, without major disruptions throughout the parent organization.

❑ The pilot effort can be used as a model for broadscale implementation.

❑ Pilot efforts are consistent with the Plan-Do-Check-Act (PDCA) approach to improvement.

❑ Develop unique plan of attack for adoption of total quality management initiative and showcase success.

Step 7. Conduct Training-Needs Analysis

Chapter 2 provides a self-assessment methodology that encourages the analysis of your organization's customer satisfaction perceptions. This self-assessment provides a baseline analysis that can be used to identify when and where you need additional training and management support.

Step 8. Determine Resources for Implementation

Your total quality management plan must disclose how the effort will be funded, where the required staff and training time will come from and how it is to be accounted for, who will provide what personnel, and what facilities will be used for total quality management. Obviously, these resource decisions must be coordinated with all those affected by the decisions. This part of the plan may be the hardest to develop because total quality management will now be competing with other requirements for business resources. One must keep in mind that total quality management is to become a way of life in your business, in fact, the new way of managing. In reality, total quality management is not competing for mission resources because it will be an integral part of the future corporate mission. This part of the plan may be the first big test of management's commitment to total quality management. Milestones for providing the identified resources should also be included in the plan.

Step 9. Conduct Training

Training is necessary for the success of your total quality management initiative. It is important to note that during the early stages of implementation of your total quality management effort, attention should be given to developing a detailed plan for training.

In addition to specific total quality management principles and practices such as statistical quality control, continuous process improvement, benchmarking, use of data, and process analysis, most business organizations will also find it necessary to conduct training in such related areas as participative management, group dynamics, problem solving, remedial skills, and team development. The ideal training program will target the specific needs of each group—top management, middle managers, supervisors, and employees in various team groups—and will deliver training "just in time" as it is needed for smooth transition to the next step in your total quality management program.

All employees must better understand their jobs and their roles in the organization, and how their jobs will change. Such understanding goes beyond the instruction given in manuals or job descriptions. Employees need to know where their work fits into the larger context: how their work is influenced by workers who precede them and how their work influences workers who follow.

The business's training plan should be an outgrowth of your unique total quality management implementation strategy, and should be directed to the organizational units or projects where top management has focused the implementation effort in the first year.

To prevent surprises and delays in implementation, the training plan must include reasonably accurate estimates of the schedule and required resources.

Step 10. Identify Performance Measures

Earlier, we discussed measuring the success of your quality improvement efforts operationally—in terms of how your customers view you, employee satisfaction, and productivity. These measure the success of your business transformation.

These key organization performance indicators are also critical to measuring the success of all total quality management activities. They are measurements that reflect the success of the total quality management improvement process. The objective of every total quality management program must be to identify performance measures for your organization, then continue to improve the key measures of success.

It is also important to measure the success of the total quality management process itself, and of the progress and implementation of each business organization's total quality management improvement plan.

THE SEVEN IMPLEMENTATION STEPS

The seven critical implementation steps, as shown in figure 6.4, can help you improve your quality by implementing a total quality management program in your organization. To begin the implementation process, the initial decision to change your emphasis to one of total quality management must have been made and the initial planning completed. Then you need to understand how your services and/or products compare with your peers. Step 12 describes the need to benchmark your performance to determine where change is needed. Then your organization must embed the continuous improvement concepts described in step 13 throughout your business. This is a major change in how your organization will operate in the 1990s. Step 14 describes the need to monitor and evaluate your progress in improving your quality performance. Tell the world of your success, but, more important, let your people know how they have contributed (step 15) to the improved operation of your business. Recognize success! As you begin to demonstrate success and convince the doubters, you must continue to learn from feedback how you can do better. You must revise or adjust your total quality management program to meet the changing needs of your organization as noted in step 16. And, finally, you must continue to improve.

Figure 6.4   Total Quality Management Implementation Steps

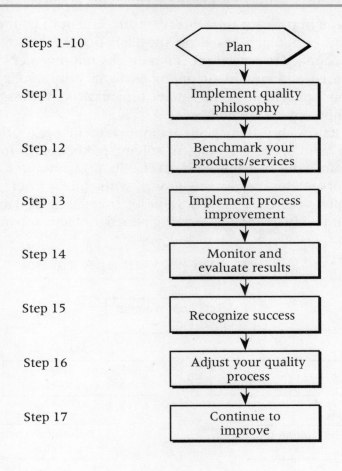

Steps 1–10	Plan
Step 11	Implement quality philosophy
Step 12	Benchmark your products/services
Step 13	Implement process improvement
Step 14	Monitor and evaluate results
Step 15	Recognize success
Step 16	Adjust your quality process
Step 17	Continue to improve

Step 11. Implement Total Quality Management Philosophy

To help you implement total quality management in your organization, an approach based on the Plan-Do-Check-Act cycle should be applied to each area of your quality improvement plan. A structured and systematic approach to identify quality improvement opportunities and resolve organization process problems is shown in figure 6.5.

The total quality management improvement cycle offers a common language and a problem-solving methodology for use throughout your organization. It facilitates communication about work under way among groups with similar interests. It also supports the basic quality value of "managing by fact" by offering individuals and teams a disciplined problem-solving ap-

Figure 6.5   A Total Quality Management Improvement Cycle

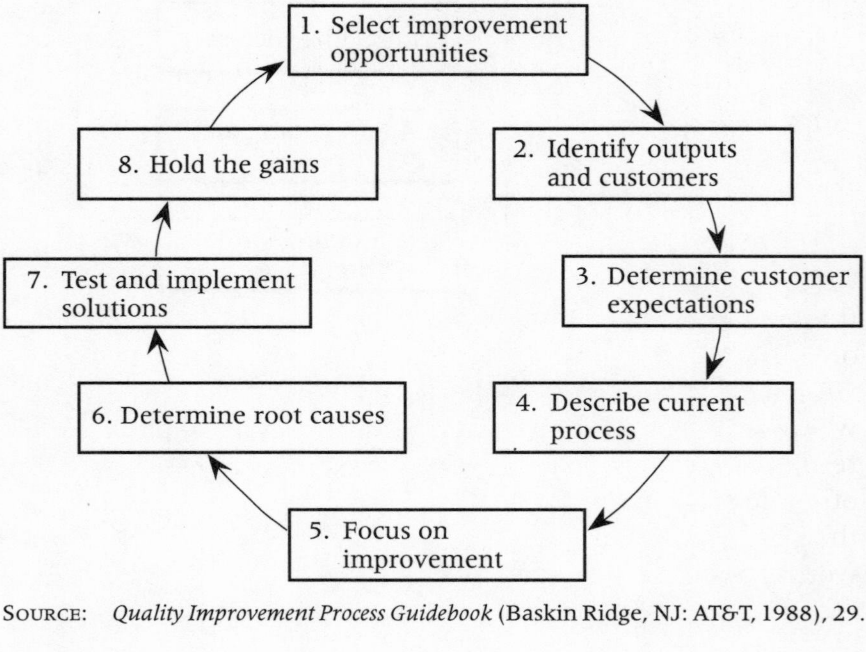

SOURCE: *Quality Improvement Process Guidebook* (Baskin Ridge, NJ: AT&T, 1988), 29.

proach. Finally, the total quality management improvement cycle increases the credibility of solutions that are developed in one part of the organization, allowing them to be readily replicated in other areas.

This cycle embodies several basic quality management theories and principles. These linkages to quality theory further assure that quality improvements projects are under way. Finally, it can assist in tracking the effectiveness of solutions in permanently eliminating root causes of quality problems.

Step 12. Benchmark Your Products/Services

In this book, we have defined "benchmark" as a standard of excellence or achievement against which other similar things must be measured or judged.

Simply speaking, benchmarking as described in great detail in chapter 4 is the process of:

- ❑ Figuring out what to benchmark.

- ❑ Finding out what the benchmark is.

- ❑ Determining how it's achieved.

- ❑ Deciding to make changes or improvements.

These four goals—while sounding fairly simple—require thinking and analysis. They require that you know your own organization processes and practices down to the smallest detail.

Benchmarking helps formulate real-world guides as to whether or not you are meeting your customers' needs. If the results of a competitive benchmarking activity show that some other organization is meeting customer requirements better, then change in your quality efforts is clearly called for. In other words, benchmarking tells you how you have met customer requirements.

Step 13. Implement Continuous Improvement Process

Continuous process improvement addresses the creation of positive change in the way work is done. It includes the definition of work flows, strengthening of supplier-customer relationships, elimination of non-value-added effort, reduction of variation, and control of processes. Continuous process improvement and process mapping are covered in detail in chapter 5.

The principles at the heart of the continuous improvement process include:

1. A constancy of purpose that provides a steady and consistent vision of where your business is going.

2. A commitment to quality that drives productive change in all the services and products you produce.

3. A customer focus and customer involvement that ensures your improvement efforts are driven by meaningful purposes.

4. Process orientation that addresses the means of work accomplishment and not just the outcomes.

5. Continuous improvement that ensures dynamic and adaptive processes over time.

6. System-centered management that ensures improvement of the whole and not just the parts.

7. Investment in knowledge that leverages the effectiveness of the improvement process.

8. Teamwork that leverages knowledge and provides essential synergy.

9. Conservation of human resources that preserves your organization's most valuable assets.

10. Total involvement that brings the entire intellectual power of your organization to bear on improvement.

11. Perpetual commitment that precludes giving up when the road gets a little rough.

These principles are applied in a logical and holistic manner to give substance and vitality to the continuously improving organizational culture. A number of the suggested readings at the end of this book examine in depth these principles and their supporting practices.

No single correct formula can be used to achieve continuous improvement in all situations or all organizations. A core set of ingredients, however, is evident in most successful continuous improvement efforts and can be applied to your own effort.

Your total quality management effort will be unique in its details, but in general it should move your organization toward satisfying the six criteria listed below.

1. Exceeding your customers' requirements and expectations and being a high-quality supplier.

2. Believing in people, working to eliminate barriers that prevent people from taking joy and pride in their work, and involving everyone.

3. Tapping the power of individuals, multiplying that power through training and teamwork and focusing it on understanding and process improvement.

4. Recognizing that most problems are in your management systems and are not due to particular individuals or circumstances, and providing leadership to improve the systems continuously.

5. Making decisions based on data rather than on opinions or emotions; stimulating creative thinking; and seeking innovation in products, processes, and services.

6. Focusing more on defect prevention than on defect detection.

Step 14. Monitor and Evaluate Results

As part of your strategy for survival, many organizations that have introduced total quality management have conducted more in-depth assessments aimed at identifying the existing culture and management style of the organization. An assessment helps to identify those vital processes to be targeted for change and provides a baseline measurement for judging progress. Assessments can take a variety of forms and frequently involve identifying and surveying the business's internal and external customers, managers, and employees. The following key considerations are often probed:

- ❑ Who are the internal and external customers?

- ❑ What measurement systems are presently in place?

- ❑ Does the organization measure its success in terms of meeting customer requirements and expectations?

- ❑ How well does the organization communicate with its customers and its suppliers?

- ❑ How much emphasis is placed on planning as opposed to "fire fighting"?

- ❑ How does the organization generate ideas for improvement? Improvement in general or quality improvement specifically?

- ❑ What type of suggestion system is in place? How effective is it?

- ❑ What does the organization reward? Improvement in general or quality improvement specifically?

- To what extent is teamwork used, encouraged, and recognized?

- What is the nature of management's relationship with employees' unions?

- How well do functional units cooperate? Are "turf" battles endemic?

- Does the executive leadership have credibility in the eyes of middle and line managers? Frontline workers?

- What type of management style is employed? Is it directive or participative?

- How much discretion do employees have in making decisions? Is authority delegated to the lowest levels possible?

- What is the attitude toward training?

- What is the attitude toward quality work? Is the focus on quality of the end product or quality of the process?

- Are the organization's values, goals, objectives, policies, and procedures clearly stated and widely known?

- Does the organization have an abundance of priorities or have a vital few been identified and articulated?

Step 15. Recognize Success

The success of total quality management is determined, in large part, by the degree of importance the organization places on it. Recognition is one of the most important ways to reinforce a proactive, positive change in behavior as it relates to quality improvement. Recognition is given for the successful application of the total quality management principles and practices.

Traditionally, rewards have been based on the "most" numbers: most revenue brought in, most profitable new product.

Total quality management, of course, also rewards bottom-line numbers. But since continuous quality improvement is a process, total quality management also provides for recognition and reward for those who demonstrate success with the processes and behaviors of total quality management—in measurable or nonmeasurable ways.

Recognition and reward are not the same things. Recognition means noticing ("recognizing") a person or group doing a good job. A manager may notice the good job at any point along its progress—not only when it is completed. Recognition usually takes the form of praise, either spoken or written. It may be as simple as a word of approval about the way an employee ran a team meeting, or as formal as a letter of commendation with copies sent to his or her management.

Recognition provides both motivation and support for employees; people work better when they feel their efforts are valued. Research has shown that such reinforcement can have a real and measurable impact on productivity.

Reward is given when the job is well done. It is tangible: usually, mementos, merchandise, stock, or cash is given. Rewards range from a simple plaque to a profit-sharing program. Rewards say, "You deserve to share in the tangible assets of your work," and as such can be powerful motivators.

Total quality management is bolstered by effective use of recognition and reward. All managers, at all levels, should continually identify those people doing a good job—and then devise ways to tell them so.

On a senior level, your business should bestow rewards and sponsor many recognition events, such as teamwork days and team excellence awards, for example.

Teamwork days are recognition events designed to honor the achievements of quality teams. Teamwork days can be held on department, division, regional, or functional levels. In addition, the organization can sponsor annual teamwork days, at which everyone in the organization is welcome to celebrate progress.

A teamwork event is like a cross between a professional conference, a trade fair, and a revival meeting. Teams create display booths, often with much ingenuity and exuberance, which showcase their accomplishments. Speakers discuss business progress in becoming a total quality management organization. People learn from each other, and the total quality management transformation grows.

The team excellence award can be a cash award given to several teams each year as a reward for implementing total quality management to achieve outstanding results. There are always more excellent teams than it is possible to reward. Recipients are chosen by senior staff, after successfully competing at division levels within their function.

Recognition and rewards should be woven into the fabric of total quality management. People who assume responsibility for continuous growth in meeting customer requirements are, in turn, motivated to further growth by honest recognition of the large role their efforts play.

Step 16. Adjust Your Total Quality Management Process

Your total quality management planning and implementation efforts must not be locked in concrete. As you learn more about your organization's strengths and weaknesses, change your total quality management efforts to reflect the feedback.

If the results are not as expected, then a new approach for improvement, based on what was learned, must be developed.

Step 17. Continue to Improve

Don't stop now! Continue to improve every facet of your business organization's operation.

CHAPTER 7

The Downsizing Trend

Downsizing, rightsizing, dumbsizing, whatever you want to call it—the "meat ax" approach to cutting costs has become a trendy thing for many business executives to implement.

You should differentiate between downsizing and reengineering, by defining "downsizing" as the arbitrary cutting of some percentage (10 to 40 percent) of your staff or budget (the downsizing method) versus an examination of your strategic business needs and operational processes (the reengineering model) to optimize your business operations so you can provide products cheaper, better, and faster than your competitors. If you are already on the verge of disaster, unfortunately you may have to join some of your peers in taking the "meat ax" approach to managing your business.

DOWNSIZING AT NYNEX CORPORATION

As described in the *Business Week* article about downsizing, which is quoted in full below, it would appear that downsizing your organization may provide the stock analysts some instant joy, but the near-term impact on your "surviving" employees in terms of trust, ability to build teams, and fully support change in your business may have downside risks that outweigh the near-term gains of the "meat ax" downsizing approach.

As described in the *Business Week* article,[1] for NYNEX Corporation,

"the bombshell fell last summer in the guise of a videotape. It was one of those slick, corporate "news" programs for employees, the kind that typically delivers some feel-good message.

Not this one. It featured a fidgeting NYNEX Corporation executive who insisted that the profitable company needed to slash its operating budget by up to 40 percent to remain competitive. The upshot: another downsizing that would eliminate fifteen thousand to twenty-five thousand people from the payroll. That meant more than one in five employees would lose their jobs. The survivors of earlier cutbacks cried foul, while management soberly tried to justify the employee meltdown.

This is the tale of what has been happening at NYNEX in the wake of that shattering announcement. It's the story of a flabby company in the midst of a gargantuan effort to remake itself, reduce costs, improve customer service, and prepare for an onslaught of more aggressive competition in the years ahead. But it is also a wrenching human drama. The players: a dynamic, steely executive leading the effort; an outside consultant whose firm is billing the company $1 million a month to help with the downsizing; a thoughtful survivor; and a resentful victim. In unusually revealing, introspective interviews, they offer an inside look at what it's really like to live through the painful process that has become a central fact of corporate life in the 1990s.

Angry and Bitter. Like many big corporations, NYNEX has been shrinking for years. Since 1990, the company has rid itself of 19,200 employees out of a total of 95,400, including 13,000 managers. In pure percentage terms, this latest cutback is one of the largest ever reported by a major corporation. The company made its plans official on January 24 by taking a $1.6 billion charge to earnings to cut 16,800 employees, or 22 percent of its workforce, over the next three years. Two months later, NYNEX acknowledged the cutbacks would cost an additional $1.3 billion in charges for severance terms more acceptable to union leaders.

Even though the company hopes to avoid forced layoffs by enticing employees to accept buyout offers, many NYNEX managers are angry and bitter. "Two months ago, I would have said that morale was low and it couldn't go any lower," says one executive. "But I'd have to say it's even lower today." Adds a former manager, "The top executives are willing to sacrifice people to make their bottom line on a quarterly basis. In the long term, they are selling the corporation out."

The drama now playing out at NYNEX is being enacted at many other corporations. Despite the economic recovery, massive downsizings continue at one brand-name behemoth after another, as shown in table 7.1. Rarely a week passes without the announcement of yet more cutbacks, in what has become the most unsettling and disruptive event in corporate America. In a quest for efficiency, companies have been charging billions of dollars off their earning to lay off hundreds of thousands of workers. The current euphemism is "downsizing" ("reengineering")—a bloodless term for corporate bloodletting on an unprecedented scale. In the year's first quarter, employers announced an average of 3,106 cut back per day.

The sight of so many bodies on the corporate scrap heap is sparking a complex debate—about profits and loyalty, and about the benefits and unforeseen consequences of layoffs. Critics, including some prominent executives, believe mas-

Table 7.1 Massive Downsizing Cuts in Corporate America

COMPANY	STAFF CUTBACKS
IBM	85,000
AT&T	83,500
General Motors	74,000
U.S. Postal Service	55,000
Sears	50,000
Boeing	30,000
NYNEX	22,000
Hughes Aircraft	21,000
GTE	17,000
Martin-Marietta	15,000
DuPont	14,800
Eastman Kodak	14,000
Philip Morris	14,000
Procter & Gamble	13,000
Phar Mor	13,000
Bank of America	12,000
Aetna	11,800
GE Aircraft Engines	10,250
McDonnell Douglas	10,200
BellSouth	10,200
Ford Motor	10,000
Xerox	10,000
Pacific Telesis	10,000
Honeywell	9,000
U.S. West	9,000

SOURCE: *People Trends* and Independent Update.

sive downsizing has become a fad, a bone to throw Wall Street when investors begin baying for cost cuts. Others maintain that large-scale staff reductions, even at profitable companies such as Procter & Gamble and Xerox, are necessary to maintain competitiveness in a fast-changing global marketplace.

Hard Choices. Few observers expect an end to the spate of downsizing announcements. "In many large companies, we still see tremendous fat," says Noel M. Tichy, a management professor at the University of Michigan. "Yet there still remains this naïve view that as the economy continues to take off, these jobs will come back. That's nonsense."

Tichy and others believe that recent gains in productivity—which rose at a 4 percent rate in the last half of 1993—are largely the result of these employee meltdowns. What the statistics of efficiency don't measure, of course, is the costs in emotional trauma to laid-off workers and their families, to the executives who often carry out the orders, or to the less-secure survivors in dramatically changed organizations.

Today's corporation is no longer a secure or stable place. It's an uncertain, turbulent environment where managers often find their compassion and humanity in conflict with the pressures of competition and ambition. Fear is almost palpable in the corridors of the downsized workplace, where loyalty takes a backseat to survival and personal advancement.

The events unfolding at NYNEX are unique, colored by the company's own culture, traditions, personalities, and politics. But they're also universal: they exemplify the challenges and the pain that face both healthy and troubled organizations everywhere.

The NYNEX Cost Cutter

Behind every major downsizing, there is a person who leads the effort, and in so doing becomes both leader and scapegoat. At NYNEX, it's Robert J. Thrasher. He's a tough-minded, fifty-one-year-old executive vice president with a history of breaking the rules.

At five feet, three inches, Bob Thrasher is a compact, muscular bundle of frantic energy—"a bionic gerbil," he jokes. Thrasher is always pacing, always talking at high-decibel level. And he's completely committed to the company: divorced from his physician wife, he typically arrives at his office at 6:45 A.M. and leaves at 7:00 P.M. He can't remember a Sunday in the past twenty years when he hasn't worked at home or in the office.

Thrasher would surely prefer to be known as the "agent of change." Instead, the executive who nervously announced the impending layoffs on that in-house video has been branded the "corporate assassin"—the person responsible for the plan to eliminate 16,800 jobs. His critics—and there are many of them—would say that he has ice water in his veins and a pocket calculator for a heart.

Since NYNEX announced its downsizing, he has had to disconnect the answering machine at his Stamford, Connecticut, home because every evening it was filled with obscene messages and threats from anonymous employees. Colleagues dub him "Thrasher the Slasher." In that same employee video, an interviewer wryly noted that he was running "unopposed as the top management SOB."

A former Air Force captain in a tactical fighter group, Thrasher insists that the tough choices he's now making are inevitable. "I know this is the right thing to do," he says. "Today, we have a virtual monopoly, but the states are in the process of opening up their markets. We have to improve service and reduce costs to stay competitive."

That realization, says Thrasher, came in mid-1992, during long-range planning discussions when he was chief operating officer of NYNEX's New York Telephone unit. Top management concluded that if it continued to run the business the same way, the company's costs per access line would keep increasing even as revenues steadily declined.

Thrasher was relieved of his chief operating officer job to head the effort to reinvent NYNEX. Why him? Many companies, from IBM to Westinghouse Electric Corporation, have sought outsiders to lead their attempts at transforming themselves. Thrasher, by contrast, is the consummate insider. He joined the company as a construction foreman in 1965, fresh out of Massachusetts Institute of Technology, where he earned a graduate degree in structural engineering. The job was in his blood: his late father was a foreman for the Niagara Mohawk Power Corporation. And what would he have thought of what his son is doing now? "My dad would have thought I'm breaking a social contract we have with our employees," Thrasher says—but then dismisses the notion. "That's the monopoly mind-set."

No one would ever accuse Thrasher of being a Bell-head, the sort of cautious bureaucrat who found shelter in the highly regulated embrace of the mother of all utilities. If anything, several associates describe him as "crazy" because of his gutsy candor and his irreverence for authority. As general manager of the company's Long Island unit in the mid-1980s, he transformed what had been one of the most troubled operations with horrendous service into one of the best. He didn't worry about bruising feelings. "In the first six months," boasts Thrasher, "I reassigned, furloughed, and forced-retired half of the senior management team there."

It was that sort of hardheadedness that made him a natural for the company-wide downsizing effort. "There was no other choice than Bob Thrasher," says Ivan G. Seidenberg, president of NYNEX. "He has enormous energy, commitment, and passion for the company. He's relentless."

Weekend Huddle. Thrasher wanted to examine the company not by division, or department, or function. Instead, he planned to analyze the company by its four core processes, which cut across the $13.4 billion corporation: customer operations, customer support, customer contact—i.e., sales and marketing—and customer provisioning, that is, the planning, design, and building of NYNEX's network. He created four teams, with a handpicked captain for each. After spending three days at GTE Corporation to get an inside look at its reengineering effort, he hired GTE's consultants, Boston Consulting Group (BCG), to help with the process at NYNEX.

By late March 1993, at a weekend meeting at the Stouffer Westchester Hotel in White Plains, New York, he put his teams together with the consultants and told his incredulous audience what he wanted: a 35 to 40 percent reduction in operating expenses. The teams, with eighty NYNEX insiders and some twenty BCG consultants in total, dispersed and rushed through the bureaucracy observing all its key operations. They visited 152 "best practice" companies, from Avis, Inc., to Virginia Power & Light, looking for useful ideas.

Back home, the inefficiencies they discovered shocked all of them—most of all, Thrasher. Among many things, he learned that NYNEX bought eighty-three brands of personal computers a year; that dozens of New York Telephone Company employees spent their time repainting newly purchased trucks a different shade of white at a cost of $500 a truck; that NYNEX spent $4.5 million to find and bill only $900,000 in previously unbillable telephone calls. There was plenty more. "Think of how embarrassed I was," says Thrasher. "I ask myself how I could have presided for two and one-half years over an operation that has been that screwed up."

His teams first came up with a list of eighty-five "quick wins"—easy fixes to make. By printing on both sides of customer bills, for example, the company will save $7 million a year on postage costs alone. By standardizing on only two personal computers, NYNEX could save $25 million in annual capital outlays. And, then, in November, came the more substantive recommendations that would lead to the massive layoffs.

All told, the four teams compiled more than three hundred specific changes, from consolidating work centers to simplifying procedures for approving customer service. Change doesn't come free, however. Thrasher initially estimated the moves would cost $700 million in expenses and $400 million in capital. But, by 1997, the changes will cut $1.5 billion to $1.7 billion from the company's $6 billion in operating expenses.

Huge Return. On three consecutive days in December—"the most excruciating days of my life"—he made presentations to the directors of three boards at NYNEX and its operating subsidiaries, New York Telephone and New England Telephone. He did something that would make any executive cringe: he asked the directors to swallow a record $1.6 billion charge against earnings and to make wholesale cuts from the payroll.

The slide that cinched the decision contained the prediction that all of Thrasher's fixes, if implemented, would generate an *internal return of 1,025 percent and a payback on investment in two years.* Thrasher told directors that if his teams could achieve only 25 percent of their goals, they would see a 226 percent return and a three-year payback. But those estimates didn't reflect the sharp increase in the actual cost of cutbacks, which had grown from $700 million in January to $2 billion two months later as a result of union negotiations.

Although he got approval to move forward—some 950 people are working to implement the changes—Thrasher still meets resistance. "Some of our senior management still don't get it," he says. "What we've got to do is find them and get them out of the business."

That's tough talk. "This is tough, ugly work," says Thrasher. "The stress is palpable. I'm vilified throughout the company. People look upon me as the principal to the downsizing. That's a tough thing to carry around. Hell, I'd like not to downsize a single employee. But that would not be a prudent decision to make."

The Downsizing Consultant

For Phillip B. Catchings, the NYNEX assignment has been the most challenging and difficult of his consulting career. As a partner at Boston Consulting Group, Catchings is the day-to-day leader of the consulting project that is costing NYNEX $1 million a month. If BCG stays at NYNEX until the job is done, the total bill could reach nearly $40 million.

Like Thrasher, he's hardly a popular figure at NYNEX these days. For one thing, employees have seen their share of high-priced consultants come and go. "NYNEX is a champion at spending millions of dollars on consultants and doing nothing with the results," grouses one manager.

Besides, every time Catchings begins a consulting assignment—and he has done about forty-five so far—he is typically met with cynicism. "There is some natural resentment when we come in," he says. "People ask, 'What makes you guys so smart?' and 'Why doesn't top management trust us to do this ourselves?' "

His job, he says, is to allay such fears—but he can't do so by pretending that his remedies will be painless. "A dentist who claims a root canal is not going to hurt will lose his credibility," he says. "I am here to do the best possible job for the organization."

Above all, of course, Catchings's presence provides shudders because he is a memento mori in pinstripes. His arrival at NYNEX or anywhere else usually means layoffs ahead. In half of his past ten assignments, he has been part of a retrenchment effort. Yet his background hardly seems to have prepared him for his role as the hardheaded, cold-hearted consultant. After graduating from Dartmouth College in 1973 with a degree in psychology, Catchings ran a foster home for delinquent teenagers. He grew a beard and long hair, bicycled across the country, and studied pottery in Washington State. The wanderlust out of his system, he spent five years in human resources with AT&T, then headed to Harvard B-school. He graduated with his M.B.A. in 1982 and went straight to BCG.

Like most consultants, he's afflicted with jargon. Catchings, forty-two, speaks of "crafting process platforms" and "deaveraging costs," of "optimum solutions" and "phase-one diagnostics." He concedes that his family is often disappointed with his inability to tell an anecdote about his work. "I must have a confidentiality filter on my brain," he says.

Along with partner Jeffrey A. Bowden, Catchings first consulted for NYNEX and Chairman William C. Ferguson in 1989. That established a relationship that led to the current assignment. Catchings, whose expertise is mainly in "change management," has spent 80 percent of his fifty-five-hour workweeks at NYNEX since late 1992. Bowden, a telecom expert, was already spearheading a similar effort at GTE that will claim seventeen thousand jobs.

Scriptwriting. The consulting pair huddled with Thrasher and other top executives once a week for four months, mapping out the project. By early March, Thrasher had picked his captains for the teams; Catchings and Bowden assembled two dozen BCG consultants. Their role: write the script for the downsizing/reengineering exercise and guide the effort.

A "compendium" of several hundred pages detailed the project's five major phases, from "direct process observation" in the first four months to "broad scale implementation," which is now under way. Catchings and Bowden helped to select the companies that teams visited for inspiration and ideas. After each trip, teams engaged in so-called clay-modeling sessions in which lessons from the visits were molded into recommendations.

Now, Catchings must get on with the painful task of building the new structure and helping to make the staff reductions that will entail. How does he reconcile himself to the job of helping others wield an ax to people, their careers, and families? "I try not to focus on that aspect of it," he says. "I'm also part of taking a frustrated, comparatively unsuccessful seventy thousand employees and transforming their environment so they can be more productive. I think I'm involved in saving lots of jobs, not destroying them."

The Survivor

Nancy P. Karen, forty-six, is pretty sure her job won't be destroyed. In her twenty-four years with the company, she has been an energetic workaholic in the critical area of information systems. As director of the company's personal-computer network, Karen is facing new and tougher demands as the result of Thrasher's efforts.

She joined New York Telephone in 1969 during the company's big bulge in hiring, often referred to as "the service glut." To meet explosive growth, the company hired tens of thousands of people in the late 1960s and early 1970s. Karen, a Vassar College graduate with a degree in math, was one of 103,000 employees at New York Telephone in 1971. Today, New York Telephone has about 40,220 people. Working in a regulated monopoly, she felt a sense of comfort and security that now seems a distant memory. "Downsizing was totally unheard of," she says. "Just about everybody here started with the company at a young age and retired off the payroll."

Thrasher's plan—and NYNEX's earlier efforts to slash the

payroll—have changed all that. Of the seventy-nine people who report directly to Karen, fifty-nine have already seen colleagues forced off the payroll in previous rounds of cut-backs. Her department is likely to suffer a 30 percent reduction in staffing. "When they started talking about another round of downsizing, people were a little more anxious because they feel they're already stretched thin. Now we'll have to learn to work smarter and completely change the way we do things."

Working smarter also means working harder—much harder. She once directly supervised twenty-six people, instead of seventy-nine, and she used to work more normal hours as well. No longer. Karen now puts in fifty to sixty hours a week, from 8:00 A.M. to 7:00 P.M. every weekday, at NYNEX's White Plains, New York, office. Wherever she goes these days, she carries a beeper and a cellular phone and checks her voice mail every hour. "It's a different mentality," she says. "My weekends and holidays are not reserved." On a recent biking vacation through California's wine country, she called the office at least once a day from "every little town." Since Karen is single, "nobody complains about my work hours," she says.

NYNEX didn't push Karen into her new and grueling pace completely unprepared. The company dispatched her to the local Holiday Inn in early 1993 for a workshop on culture change put together by Senn-Delaney Leadership, a Long Beach, California, consulting firm.

She was skeptical at first. "To me, it was yet another program," she says. Surprisingly, Karen left a believer. The sessions—dubbed Winning Ways—are an effort to inculcate the new values and skills that NYNEX believes it needs to make Thrasher's downsizing/reengineering changes take hold. It's a quick-and-dirty roundup of today's managerial commandments, stressing teamwork, accountability, open communications, respect for diversity, and coaching over managing.

Although impressed by how the sessions encouraged employees to speak more freely to each other, Karen saw her share of nonconverts at the initial two-and-one-half-day meeting. "Some people come back to work unchanged," she says. "But there's a big middle section that seems willing to change, and then there's a small percentage at the top that's very enthusiastic about it."

Brain Drain? Not that Karen, who earned an M.B.A. from Columbia University on the company's tab in 1981, doesn't have some big worries about the change effort. One of them is that the downsizing will get ahead of the company's ability to figure out ways to get the work done more efficiently. She's also worried that the company will lose expertise and talent. That would mean that she and other managers won't have enough of the right people to accomplish the tasks placed before them. "It's not going to work perfectly," she says. "There will be cases when the downsizing occurs before the reengineering."

Despite the increased workload and her concern over employee morale, Karen considers herself lucky. "This is a wonderful challenge," she says. "I'm looking at a task of building a new organization in the next six months to a year. I have the chance to test myself as I've never been tested before."

The Victim

Not everyone shares Karen's optimistic view of life at NYNEX. Uncertainty and fear loom over many. When NYNEX began sending out details of the buyout packages to some workers in New England, employees knew that if enough people refused the package, the company would be forced to push them out.

Many are understandably bitter. They feel as if they are

victims of some abstract management exercise beyond their control or even their capacity to understand. One of them, an urbane manager with more than twenty years of experience, expects to pounce on an early-retirement package, to walk out, and start a new phase of life. "This company's values have changed," the manager says. "There are now right people and wrong people here, and I don't believe in that."

Fearful of retribution, this employee doesn't want to be identified. But Pat, as we'll call this middle manager in a staff position, is remarkably candid about the turmoil inside the company. Pat has made presentations before Bob Thrasher and thinks he's a "brilliant, if ruthless, executive. As an officer of the company, he's very focused and clearly sees the possibilities." But this NYNEX veteran doesn't see Thrasher and other top managers sharing the pain. "The officers all have golden parachutes. They're in charge of their own fates. We're not involved. We're just affected."

Looking at the fate of the managers and employees who lost their jobs in NYNEX's earlier cutbacks, Pat can see the profound changes that may lie ahead. Many are still without work. More than 150 of them have joined a class action against the company, alleging that they were selected for dismissal because of age discrimination.

Although the company formally announced its latest round of cutbacks three months ago, not a single employee has yet lost a job. Details of buyout offers, including accelerated pensions, are being sent to employees in selected business units. Thrasher says the buyout offer "removes the anxiety and angst in the workforce."

Not to this middle manager, who believes offering incentives to quit isn't that much different from terminating employees outright with severance pay. "Even if people won't be fired this time, they're still frightened of the future. It affects their self-esteem and their pocketbook. And most people aren't going from something to something. They have no place to go."

Values Lost. Sure, Pat fears for a job that may be lost. But, mostly, Pat claims to fear that the company to which this middle manager's professional life has been devoted will never recover from the bloodletting. Pat recalls taking hours to walk to work in the aftermath of a major snowstorm—a degree of commitment employees won't be likely to feel in the future. This manager wonders if the repairmen who now rush to set up emergency communications lines at the scene of incidents such as the bombing of the World Trade Center will move less urgently because of NYNEX's perceived lack of loyalty to its employees. Corporate values that not long ago focused on caring for employees have been rewritten so that now employees come last, Pat says, after shareholders and customers.

The Draconian downsizing, Pat believes, is really a knee-jerk response to a complex set of problems that might be addressed more subtly. "Other companies, like Hewlett-Packard, have refocused their strategy, cleaned up their product and service lines, and for the most part retrained their folks without massive layoffs, and they're doing exceptionally well."

Such humane options, however, may be for executives and companies that don't have to cut as deeply or as thoroughly as NYNEX. As everyone involved would concede, the pain of this massive downsizing isn't likely to go away any time soon."

THERE IS AN UP SIDE TO DOWNSIZING[2]

Next to the death of a relative or friend, there's nothing more traumatic than losing a job, as shown in table 7.2.

Corporate cutbacks threaten the security and self-esteem of survivors and victims alike. Layoffs disrupt careers and families. They cause turmoil and shatter the morale inside organizations. And they confirm the public's view that profits always come before people.

So it comes as no surprise that when consulting firms survey human resource executives about recent downsizings, they find some negative results. Indeed, study after study appears to prove that the downside of downsizing often outweighs any savings the cutbacks produce. Management underestimates the costs to slash workers and the impact cutbacks have on the morale of survivors. "People become preoccupied with layoffs," says John J. Parkington, a consultant with Wyatt Company, which published a significant downsizing, as "People spend more time on internal politics, they become less productive."

Table 7.2 The Traumatic Impact of Downsizing

1. Death of spouse

2. Divorce

3. Marital separation from mate

4. Detention in jail or other institution

5. Death of a close family member

6. Major personal injury or illness

7. Marriage

8. **Being fired at work**

9. Marital reconciliation

10. *Retirement from work* (planned or forced)

SOURCE: Adapted with permission from the *Journal of Psychosomatic Research*, vol. II. "The Social Readjustment Scale," T. H. Holmes and R. H Rahe. Pergamon Press, 1967.

Bad Press. In truth, downsizing has gotten something of a bum rap. Parkington's own study shows that 77 percent of the executives Wyatt surveyed believe that restructuring had a positive impact on productivity. Only 13 percent considered the impact adverse. Sure, morale suffered in the short term. But the mood does pick up, especially when cutbacks are combined with efforts to reduce bureaucracy. Other benefits from downsizing were cited by the survey's respondents: enhanced quality and customer service and greater willingness among survivors to take risks, perhaps because of accompanying efforts to encourage them to be more venturesome.

Yet another survey by the American Management Association claimed that downsizing's goals of increased profits and greater productivity continue to prove elusive. The survey gathered these views, however, from human resource managers, who are far more likely to view cutbacks in a highly negative light. And even the human resource managers said profits declined at only one in five companies downsized since early 1988.

Another study by three professors at the University of Wisconsin also generated bad press for (downsizing) layoffs. The report contends that a company's financial performance worsens two years after the announcement of a downsizing. Although there's often a short-term advantage to layoffs, any gains in profit margins and return on equity disappear two years after the announcement.

THE REAL PICTURE

Study after study contends that companies commonly underestimate the costs of downsizing and often fail to gain the expected efficiencies. But the studies have their faults, too.

- Financial performance worsens two years after a company announces a massive layoff, according to a 1993 study by three academics at the University of Wisconsin. Though there is often a short-term advantage to downsizing, any gains in profit margins and return on equity soon disappear.

- Fewer than half the companies that downsize meet the financial and operational goals they set for themselves, according to a 1993 study by Wyatt Company. Morale was hurt in 56 percent of the 531 surveyed.

- This Wyatt Company study of only seventeen companies that announced layoffs in 1989 is hardly definitive. The authors reviewed 1991 financial results that were adversely affected by the recession. Many of these troubled companies would have been even worse off if they hadn't reduced costs through cutbacks.

- The report also found that downsizing led to such positive changes as improved productivity, enhanced quality and customer service, and a greater willingness among survivors to take risks.

Dig behind these headline-grabbing conclusions, however, and you find some remarkable information. The Wyatt Company study is based on seventeen companies that announced layoffs in 1989. Because the authors chose to study companies immediately after they announced cutbacks, rather than after the layoffs took place, they may give a distorted view.

"A lot of these companies are poorly managed concerns that got in trouble," says Noel M. Tichy, a management professor at the University of Michigan. "If they refused to lay off people, they would report bigger losses or go bankrupt." Concedes Kenneth P. De Meuse, one author of the study: "There may be a chicken-and-egg thing here."

In other words, there's no telling whether the deteriorating results are the consequence of the layoffs, or—as is more likely—merely the further playing out of the business woes that sparked the downsizing in the first place. Two years may not be long enough to see results. Indeed, if De Meuse and his colleagues had extended their period of review, they also would have found sizable rises in net income and profit margins at other companies in the study, including Boeing, Chrysler, Hewlett-Packard, Motorola, and Texas Instruments.

These companies are among those that have aggressively cut costs and changed the way work is done. When John F. Welch became chief executive of General Electric Company in 1981, the company employed nearly 420,000 people. Today, some 222,000 are on the GE payroll, yet the company has tripled its net profits and more than doubled its revenues. "I know that GE made a bundle of money out of downsizing," adds Tichy, co-author of a book on Welch. "If you figure that each person with salary and benefits costs about $60,000 a year, that means GE has taken $18 billion out of its cost structure."

Make no mistake: "downsizing is hardly a quick fix. It is not a strategy, and it is not a panacea for poor management. Healthy companies that slash payrolls instead of devising new game plans for growth are sending a demoralizing message to employees. Massive layoffs should be avoided when possible through shorter workweeks, wage and hiring freezes, and cutbacks in executive perks. But the idea that downsizing can't sometimes be an effective way for bloated, uncompetitive companies to cut costs is pure nonsense."

SO YOU REALLY WANT TO DOWNSIZE

"We just address the symptoms and not the cause!" This is the frustrated cry of every executive who has just implemented a decision to improve his or her organization and found that it either didn't work, wasted resources, or exacerbated the real problem. All too often managers are called upon to make decisions to improve their organizations, be it in the area of cost cutting, downsizing, efficiency and productivity improvements. And yet these decisions are often made in the absence of reliable, objective, and comprehensive information. If you are faced with critical financial, competitive, or organizational problems, you should begin your actions by assessing where your business is and what you have to do to survive.

The purpose of a downsizing assessment is to provide you and your senior team with a solid base from which to view your business, by gathering relevant real performance and competitive benchmarking data and converting it into simple comprehensible and practical action plans.

Tolstoy once said that all unhappy families are unhappy in their own way; all happy families are happy in the same way. In a similar way, healthy organizations adopting significant change all seem to possess comparable characteristics, including:

1. Primary business survival goals of your business, and the reason you must change, are clear and effectively communicated to every employee.

2. The business strategy or approach that is followed for reaching your goals is well developed, adhered to, and modified as needed.

3. The core technology (information systems and automation) is sufficient to allow you to meet your goals.

4. All the principal roles and responsibilities of your subordinates, required to implement change, have been well defined.

5. Management systems are in place or are being developed that redefine all work processes to enable the effective implementation of your downsizing strategy.

6. There must be agreement by the board and the senior executive that the necessary financial resources to support the full impact of change will be available.

7. Dynamic, gutsy, consistent, no-holds-barred leadership is mandatory to see near-term performance improvement and business survival.

These characteristics are all interlinked in such a way that deficiencies in one characteristic will usually show up in others. For example, if the system for employee communication is not well developed or is flawed, interpersonal and team relationships will usually suffer. If the basic strategy is poorly conceived, then your goals may not be reached. And so on.

Therefore, in attempting to understand the problems that face your business, it is important to look at the entire range and relationship among survival characteristics to identify the primary factors or bottlenecks that are contributing to problems. One of the things that can make this kind of internal analysis difficult for executives is that he or she is a part of the failing organization. Membership in the system automatically makes it difficult to be fully objective and detached adequately to see the whole realistic picture.

For this reason, executives, as in the case of NYNEX, often seek an outside consultant to help them better understand their organization and assist in conducting independent assessments of what could be changed to help assure your survival. Before discussing how a consultant would work, let's first consider what kind of circumstances would prompt a manager to begin a downsizing assessment.

WHEN SHOULD YOU DOWNSIZE?

A downsizing assessment is an opportunity to stand back and take a global look at the strengths and weaknesses of your business, and determine the problems you must overcome to compete in the changing market. It is especially important to conduct a downsizing assessment when:

- Your company is on the verge of going out of business due to national economic cyclic declines, financial failures or mismanagement by your predecessor, loss of market share, or introduction of new competitive products that will destroy your product or service base.

- Your business organization and process problems are seriously impacting productivity, efficiency, or employee commitment.

- Consequences of near-term management leadership inaction or business management failure are severe.

- There are multiple and/or interrelated contributing factors such as corporate acquisitions or mergers confronting your business.

Certainly, as a leader in your business, you need to weigh a variety of factors in deciding whether or not you are at the point at which you must downsize your organization to survive, or if you need to examine the potential of downsizing to assure that your competitors' cost- and people-cutting actions do not render your business less competitive. However, the most important question to consider is how useful the assessment will be. And, in most cases, the value of your downsizing assessment will depend on the process that is used for conducting it.

Elements of Successful Downsizing Assessment

The most successful downsizing assessments are those in which:

- Critical problems or concerns have been identified by your management team that require immediate action.

- A consultant team is selected whose members have experience in radical change in businesses like yours, are well grounded in change management, process simplification and process improvement, organization assessment and analysis, and group dynamics.

- Time and resources are committed that enable management to take an active role in planning, data analysis, and action planning.

- Follow-through occurs on all key actions that are made.

Most executives are particularly concerned about the time and cost requirements of conducting such an assessment:

- The time requirements will vary considerably depending on factors such as: size of the organization, number of sites involved, method to be followed, availability of executives and consultant support, and scope of assessment.

- The financial costs of the assessment will also vary widely depending on whether an internal or external consultant is used, and the specific form and scope of data gathering that is decided upon.

- No matter what your initial estimates (30 to 40 percent of your time) are for the impact of downsizing on your personal involvement and time, it will take more time than you anticipated. Downsizing, like other change issues, is very difficult, consumes time and strength, and is not very much fun! Carefully consider if this is what you must do to have your business survive.

HOW TO DOWNSIZE YOUR BUSINESS

All too often one hears about a downsizing or organizational assessment sitting unread on some executive's bookshelf.

Usually this is either because top management has not fully subscribed to the downsizing assessment process, or after understanding the downsizing report, the leadership finds that it does not have the stomach or will to embark on such painful change, or the consultant's findings lacked credibility.

To avoid these sorts of problems, a downsizing assessment should be done as a collaborative relationship between the executive leadership and your consultant, where you actively participate in setting the agenda for the assessment and in interpreting the results.

While initially the top executive orders the full-blown assessment, this role often broadens to encompass a group such as the senior management team and, as the effort progresses, a representation of employees and other managers. This larger group can provide a broader perspective for interpreting results, as well as ensure greater support for decisions and commitment to follow through.

The basic method for this approach to downsizing assessment follows these steps:

1. Executive and consultant (either outside or inside consulting resource) define (a) the purpose and scope of the downsizing assessment, (b) the critical business operation areas that should receive special process focus, and (c) the methods to be used for gathering data; methods may include benchmarking—internal and external; in-depth operational staff interviews; product, process, or productivity surveys; independent examination of documents and reports; or a combination of these critical data points.

2. Consultant gathers and organizes data to summarize the scope of the needed changes, and develops a road map or process map to define what must be changed, and provides options for management review and action.

3. Consultant presents in several corporate forums his or her recommendations to management. This material is re-

viewed in detail and management requests clarification, more specific information, or identifies critical issues that need more examination. Management decides to proceed with their downsizing effort or hold action till conditions justify change.

4. If downsizing is required for business survival, the consulting and management team revises the implementation plans to reflect near-term actions to assure business survival.

5. Your management team implements action plans.

6. A reassessment, after the first year of action has been started, is conducted to determine impact of changes.

Downsizing may not be fun, but if you have waited too long to revitalize your business, it may be the only course of action available to show your financial sponsors that you are aggressively embarking on a business improvement and survival effort.

CHAPTER 8

Reengineer Your Business

Reengineering is often symbolized as the word for "radical change" in the nineties. Do you wonder why your business should be or is going through such change that is turning many businesses upside down? Chapter 7 described the trendy downsizing activities that are often linked to reengineering. Although downsizing is causing great disruption in business, and downsizing and reengineering are often linked or addressed as one and the same process, this chapter views reengineering in a more positive light, focusing on product and process reengineering.

Reengineering can be used to help simplify your processes, improve productivity, and in an evolutionary manner provide the opportunity for your employees to take on entirely new job responsibilities as your business is turned around and begins to grow again.

WHY REENGINEER?

In order to satisfy your customers, you must develop new products cheaper, better, and faster (the CBF factor) than you did last year. You should examine the potential of reengineering your processes to assure that your competitors, by significantly changing the way they do business, won't surprise you in the competitive game of survival.

Businesses do not reengineer their processes just to cut costs, according to a Grant Thornton study noted in table 8.1. This survey of chief executive officers uncovered several important motivations to reengineer your business.

Table 8.1 Motivations to Reengineer

MOTIVATOR	PERCENT
Reduce costs	84
Improve quality	79
Increase speed (throughput)	62
Overcome a competitive threat	50
Change the organizational structure	35
Other	9

In response to these motivational interests, organizations are implementing various functional changes by improving process flows, investing in automation, organizing operations by customer or product line, and bringing the management communication levels closer together.

Reengineering is a state-of-the-practice management approach that applies the "best practices," process simplification principles, analytical tools, and management techniques to help assure your survival in this very competitive marketplace. Reengineering concentrates on examining the ways you can significantly improve your business by replacing, deleting, or improving your processes.

Quality-based reengineering is a management approach in which system defects are avoided rather than corrected later in the process. The potential of reengineering is tremendous, if properly conceived and implemented.

Reengineering provides an optimum application of people and technology to (1) produce new products, (2) enhance existing products and processes, (3) improve your business enterprise, administrative support, engineering, and manufacturing processes. The significance of reengineering is to create a new way of satisfying your customers' needs.

As shown figure 8.1, the greatest opportunities for reengineering are in the following areas:

- Functional "process" reengineering—65 percent

- "Product" reengineering—23 percent

- Corporate-wide "business process reengineering" (BPR)—12 percent

Many consulting companies are trying to sell the idea that every business must be totally reexamined and reengineered. Based on Technology Research Corporation's "cultural change" management experience, we can only identify a small number of companies that will totally reengineer their business enterprise. The problems with radical corporate-wide reengineering recommendations are as follows:

- Companies will only take the radical enterprise-wide reengineering path if they are *forced to change*.

- The culture change requires too much time and commitment for top management to stay the course. Often, consul-

Figure 8.1   Potential Reengineering Opportunities

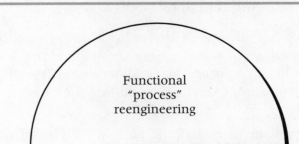

tants sell "reengineering" as a quick fix for business success, but significant bottom line performance improvements take at least eighteen months.

- ❑ If your business has a history of not being able to implement any new business management system, it is unlikely that you will be able to adopt radical corporate-wide business process reengineering (BPR) without major disruption.

- ❑ Executives often rely on "peer experience" for new management systems, before they will take the risk of change. They are unwilling to attempt massive change unless they know that it has worked, or their path to survival has no other alternative approach.

- ❑ Very few companies have adopted the radical business process reengineering for all of their corporation's products and processes. There are too few "total" application success stories available today to turn your business over to an outside guru for radical change.

❑ Very few, if any, of the radical business processing reengineering consultants have created and implemented radical business process reengineering (BPR) for an entire organization like yours, including their own.

The good news is that the basic principles of reengineering (asking why we are developing products or processes the way we have been) is very useful for "new product" reengineering, and functional "process" reengineering. The potential for reengineering your processes, where you reexamine the product or process, with a new vision for the type and extent of alternate approaches has been clearly demonstrated. Pilot demonstrations of "product" and "process" reengineering efforts can help convince your team that it will benefit your business.

Present reality is, in a word, change. The world has never changed so fast as in the present century, and change will escalate in the future. Present reality demands quality, value, reliability, and consumer satisfaction; and your customers want all of these perfection goals at a lower cost.

Top management leaders, co-workers, suppliers, machinery builders, information system wizards, product design specialists, resource managers, marketers, and every one of your employees must play an active role in your reengineering effort if it is to be really successful. As described in chapter 7, there are winners and losers, and survivors that are part of your reengineering transition. The only way to succeed is to understand and evaluate your strategic processes so they can be improved from end to end. The reengineering process shown in figure 8.2 identifies an optimum management systems approach that can produce the desired product or service, that has the required level of quality, is delivered in a predetermined time, within a preset cost.

To survive in the changing market, American business leaders are beginning to recognize the advantages of reengineering. The concept of reengineering as used in this book is a shorthand way of stressing two fundamental tenets:

- Reengineering of "products" and "processes" should become part of your business survival strategy. Reengineering takes considerable top management attention and persistence. If you have world-class quality products, services, and people, you will also generate world-class profits, and survive in this rapidly changing market.

- Your business's reengineering program must address its own unique needs. Off-the-shelf, "just add water" canned reengineering solutions cannot generate the level of human commitment within your business that is needed for you to succeed. In fact, you may substitute your business's reengineering initiative name (Business Process Redesign, Inspire, Team Zebra, or Rapid Product Realization) in place of the term "reengineering" when thinking about some of the concepts presented in this book.

WHAT IS REENGINEERING?

Reengineering is a fundamentally new way of looking at how products and processes are changed from conception to customer delivery and satisfaction.

For products, development has been described as a sequential process. Traditional product design and development have been characterized as separate functional units (such as product design and manufacturing production) that pass their new products "over the wall" to the next isolated functional area in the development and production process. Communication among functional units is very formal, and interdepartment boundaries limit effective communication. Each functional group sees the

Figure 8.2 Process-Driven Improvement

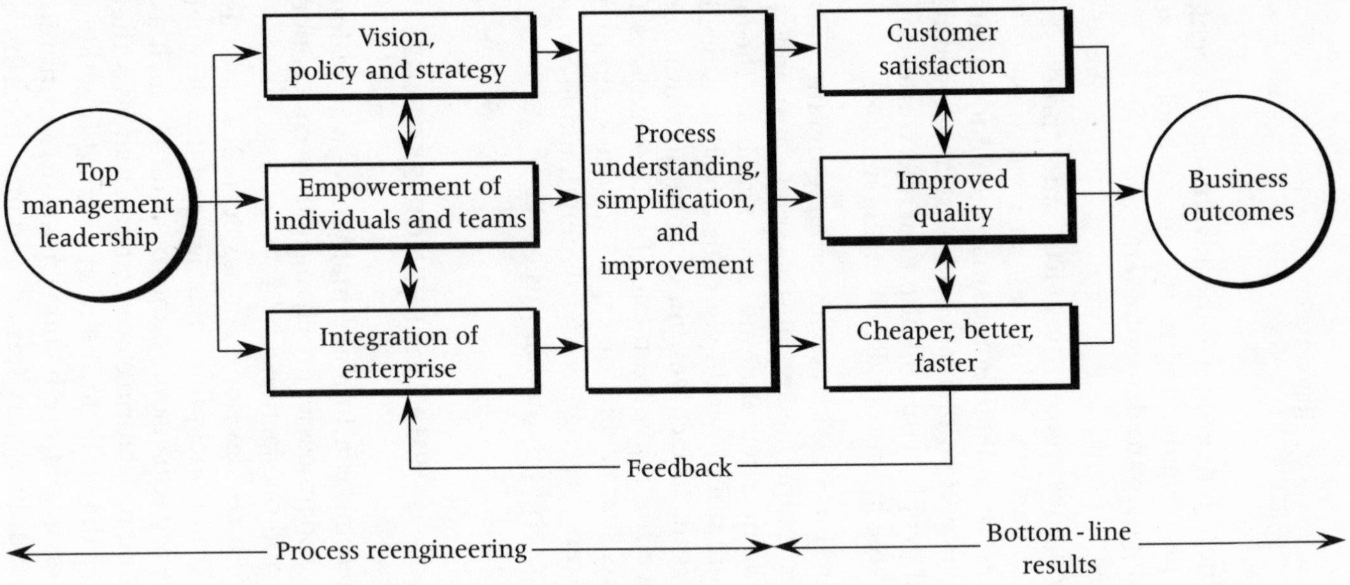

new product only after the preceeding group is finished with its own functional efforts. The traditional sequential product development process becomes progressively less efficient as product complexity, organization complexity, and global market demand increase. Reengineering reflects the synthesis and application of the best product development methods available today in America.

Figure 8.3 illustrates the basic elements of reengineering your "products" and "processes." It is focused on outcomes (profit improvement, defect reduction, faster product development cycles, etc.) that directly affect the competitiveness of your business. The fundamental elements of reengineering stress:

1. *Customer satisfaction.* Reengineering requires your managers to understand what your customers want, and helps you define product or service requirements that will satisfy your customers.

2. *Process understanding.* Most new product development efforts are hindered when your business management, product engineers, manufacturing engineers, and business enterprise improvement teams do not understand all the process elements from product conception to product support. Before radical reengineering, you need to benchmark and identify your product and process strengths and weaknesses. To arbitrarily throw "the baby out with the bathwater" does not solve your near-term business survival or growth needs. If a radical reengineering of your product development was done, without understanding your corporate processes, you might reinvent the original organizational development problems.

3. *Radical reengineering.* According to Dr. Michael Hammer and James Champy in their book *Reengineering the Corporation*, from 50 to 75 percent of the organizations that undertake radical business process reengineering do not achieve the dramatic results they expected.[1] Some recommend "radical" change in terms of questioning everything that is done and trying to determine if

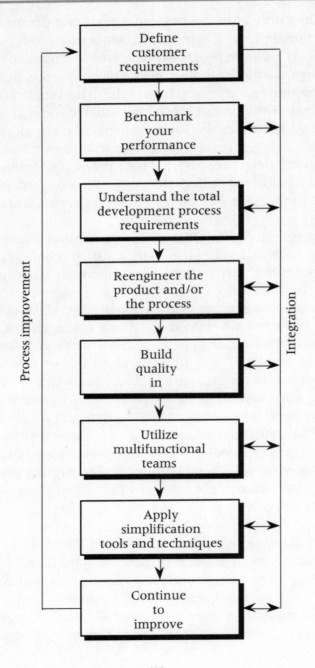

it should have been done. Business process reengineering questions the total enterprise-wide and individual processes involved in satisfying the development of new products for your customers. However, for all the management books and press hype, few corporations will turn their business over to an outside consultant to radically change the way they do business. Rather than risk major implementation failures by adopting radical enterprise-wide change for near-term action, you should carefully explore business process reengineering and downsizing options to assure successful adoption.

4. *Quality goals.* One concept that your near-term efforts must focus on is quality-driven "bottoms-up" team participation in your reengineering effort. The vision for your business must include quality stretch goals, such as Motorola's Six Sigma approach, or more specific product development quality metrics. Today's quality goals concentrate on reducing variation in processes and measurement systems. Your reengineering effort should be characterized as focusing on product and process elimination, process simplification and integration, process improvement, teamwork, and total quality management, and your active leadership participation in change.

5. *Adoption of multifunctional teams.* The only way to unleash the power of reengineering is to create multifunctional teams that include, rather than exclude, all of the relevant process units within your business. New products or services that satisfy the cheaper, better, faster requirements of your customers is "good business." New product development teams must include all the "product" and "process" owners, from purchasing through customer service to assure customer satisfaction.

Teamwork is important for successful reengineering implementation. The process improvements from each project contribute toward the total process improvement. Both management and the organizational structure must promote team activities. No longer can you effectively dictate all activities within your business. Your management system should be changing to focus more on participative management and teamwork.

In these quality-based approaches, the organizational structure flattens, as noted in chapter 7. Strict functional alignments found in vertically structured organizations are removed and the organization becomes more unified. Flatter organizational structures promote cross-functional teamwork to address issues and processes that impact the entire organization. Less restrictive communication results from removing barriers between work areas. Employees can work together to improve the supplier-customer relationships. A flatter organizational structure also improves communication through the organizational hierarchy; management listens to what the teams are saying rather than telling them to "listen up" during one-way, downward-directed communications.

Reengineering requires a team approach to new "product" and "process" design. Technology is important to efficiently design, and utilize, increasingly complex systems; but technology is not the total answer to improving your process. Without any computer or special software, you can today, with pencil and paper, identify what the major problems and critical "bottleneck" problems are that you need to address.

Early conceptual or "systems" thinking involves many issues, thus it requires a multidisciplined team, pulled from across the entire organization and chartered to address issues impacting the overall system life cycle. While early details may often preclude detailed decision making due to risk and uncertainty in the eventual system characteristics, issues such as support, maintenance, manpower, personnel, and training should be considered early to avoid later conflicts as your new system evolves and the system characteristics become more defined. This reengineering team approach requires a product teaming organizational structure characterized by open communication among team members, access to evolving design information, clear and concise reporting channels to management, and commitment to the project versus commitment to the functional "home" office.

The reengineering multifunctional team concepts can also be applied to contract-subcontractor relationship as organizations work together to improve their product and processes. The better the subcontractors' products in terms of conformance to specifications, quality of workmanship, and adaptability to your system, the more efficient and effective your operation shall be. Working as a team to communicate effectively your requirements of the system development project allows for an efficient subcontractor-to-contractor flow of products or services. This in turn enhances the systems and integration process to ultimately improve the quality of the products or services delivered to your customers.

6. *Tools, and Techniques.* Knowledge about individual reengineering tools (such as work-flow analysis), and techniques (such as process mapping) does not constitute understanding of, nor create the management leadership that facilitates change. Each tool must be viewed in terms of the synergistic benefit possible when it is combined, integrated, or uniquely applied to improve your processes. Tools and techniques are process improvement aids that can help you to facilitate change.

Because every business is unique, you will have to be the change agent. You will have to understand these new tools and techniques, and then select and apply them for your own reengineering processes.

7. *Continue to improve the process.* Management must recognize that all reengineering efforts are made up of process understanding, process simplification, and effective change management to significantly improve the way you have done business.

Any organization, whether a manufacturing firm, a service organization, or a consulting firm, accomplishes its mission via processes. Within these processes are the "hidden operational processes." These "hidden operational processes" costs your business money without generating income or adding any value. Reducing the unrecognized costs of your "hidden operational processes" by eliminating, simplifying, or improving your work processes clearly increases profits. A climate of process improvement evolves through an ongoing focus on the work processes. Each worker and co-worker should be knowledgeable in their work process and those processes that affect their own process. This will provide them the ability to ask and address the question: "Is there a better way?" Management must allow workers to openly question the current standards, and form teams to examine and improve the work processes. With the increased emphasis on improving the cheaper, better, factor (CBF) must also come the realization that true increases in performance result from eliminating the need for the process. Furthermore, by continuing to improve the work processes, management can build flexibility into the organization; flexibility needed to cope with rapid change caused by increasing systems complexity and changing technology.

Reengineering brings tremendous potential to the development process.

Reengineering can also be characterized by focus on the customer's requirements and priorities, a conviction that quality is the result of improving the product and process, and a philosophy that improvement (radical, revolutionary, or evolutionary) of all the processes of design, production, and support are never-ending responsibilities of the entire enterprise. The building blocks of reengineering are not new. The terms "system engineering," "simultaneous engineering," "concurrent engineering," and "process value engineering" have long been used to describe portions of reengineering.

The integrated examination of your products and processes is the key to reengineering. Reengineering seeks to improve the total business processes by the functional integration of your processes.

Your business is capable of fully implementing reengineering now! Implementation can be based on a simple reengineering strategy.

❏ Eliminate, simplify, or integrate organizations, products, processes, and activities based on reengineering principles, eliminating "stovepiping" and "over-the-wall" transactions through the use of multifunctional teams.

❏ Establish active top management leadership for enterprise-wide reengineering.

❏ Rethink how your business addresses gaining a better understanding of both co-worker and customer needs.

❏ Implement a process that will lead to the use of appropriate tools (work-flow analysis) to improve process integration.

UNIQUE CHARACTERISTICS OF REENGINEERING

Table 8.2 provides a generic delineation of the unique characteristics of reengineering.

Table 8.2 Unique Reengineering Characteristics

❏ Focuses on eliminating, understanding, simplifying, and bundling business processes, to improve your productivity and significantly reduce operational costs.

❏ Optimizing the suite of product and processes in a systematic, integrated, comprehensive, phased, and practical manner.

❏ Establishing product and process customer satisfaction criteria based upon customer needs.

❏ Provides better understanding of your internal and external logistics and support requirements, and their integration in your total business needs.

Figure 8.4 illustrates reengineering's unique emphasis on people, process, and technology. People are the critical mass in terms of reengineering implementation. More than 50 percent of your reengineering effort is tied to your management leadership, and team member and co-worker understanding of how you can implement multifunctional process assessment teams and emphasize total quality management to effect change in your business. Approximately 45 percent of your reengineering effort is process elimination, process understanding, and process simplification driven; and the balance of 5 percent is use of new or better process analysis technology.

Beware of the technology salesmen! We do not require any new technology today to gain significant benefits from reengineering. As figure 8.4 shows, the two key implementation elements are applying multifunctional process assessment teams (50 percent), and adopting total quality management (25 per-

Figure 8.4   Reengineering Emphasis on People, Process, and Technology

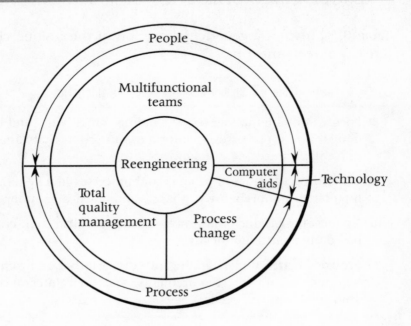

cent) principles to evaluate and significantly change your business processes.

PITFALLS OF REENGINEERING

The benefits of reengineering are substantial, but they are not easily achieved. The most important lessons learned in the implementation of reengineering are noted below.

Top management commitment in the form of learning, understanding, and leading your reengineering efforts with unwavering direction and constant management involvement, as described in chapter 7, is absolutely vital to your success. The many process improvements and cost savings that result from reengineering are due mostly to the application of multifunctional process examination teams, willingness to manage change, and the use of quality improvement techniques.

But the really impressive savings (potentially, hundreds of millions of dollars, depending on the size of your business) remain largely unrecognized because they result only from reengineering improvements of the larger "management systems" and "operational choices" over which only top management has control. These larger systems include strategic policies of your business, such as elimination of whole marginal business entities, reduction of marginally profitable product lines, corporate willingness to foster better working relationships with your suppliers, improving the adversarial relationships with employees or unions, providing for pay-for-performance or special skills, adopting new compensation policies to reward performance, reducing turf battles between other elements of your corporate world, and presenting a constant message to all your change agents. To date, those reengineering efforts that have failed are due to the inability of top management to comprehend, and to actively execute, their reengineering initiative. Their verbal "support" for reengineering is simply not enough!

Your reengineering effort must be led. One corporation's lack of leadership for reengineering adoption has resulted in a "new" effort without any clear direction or guidance within divisions and between the divisions. This fosters the widespread perception that reengineering is a fad that will eventually go away. In contrast, the efforts under way at Chrysler, Ford Motor Company, Motorola, Hallmark, Xerox, United Parcel Service, Capital Holding, Bell Atlantic, and other companies are well directed and guided because of top management leadership, starting with the chairman of the board.

Most companies place too much emphasis on the techniques of reengineering and not enough emphasis on the critical management system philosophy underlying the application of the techniques. This partly explains the lack of top management understanding and involvement. Some top managers view reengineering as something the corporate strategic planners can conceive and implement on their own. Reengineering is more a management system than just a bag of tools, techniques, and tricks!

Some businesses have ushered through continuous "waves" of new management techniques over the past several years, fueling the perception that reengineering is a coming-and-going fad. These techniques have included quality circles, value engineering, zero-base budgeting, management by objectives, and many others. Your people are confused about what they ought to be doing today to help assure the survival of their company and their jobs.

Management should focus more on the reengineering management system integration concepts in their initial rollout, and then follow through with the tools and techniques. This would provide a sound baseline for guiding your reengineering teams' effort. Because they did not do this, some people still view reengineering as a bunch of techniques that may or may not apply in the "same old way" management environment. So far, the fact that these techniques are powerful and profitable is not sufficient to ensure their successful proliferation.

Many enterprises facing destruction begin implementing re-engineering without having a workable plan of attack. They just want "to do it now"! Consequently, the reengineering staff tries to apply the techniques with little upper management understanding and guidance. Upper management does not know how to support the efforts. They do not quite understand what their responsibility is, nor what questions they should ask. The end results may be that many attempts sputter along, then stop, leaving a bad taste with everyone. If they were to start completely over again, the best approach would be to have top management take whatever time was necessary for them to learn and understand the impact of such massive change on their organization, talk with their executive peers in other companies that have gone through the painful process of reengineering their business: then, top management can try to better understand their responsibility; develop their purpose, vision, direction, and plan for implementing the effort business-wide; and then execute and continuously communicate their plans.

These are some of the pitfalls your peers have recognized. Try to understand fully the culture change, cost, personal effort, and derived outcome before you commit your enterprise to reengineering.

STATE-OF-THE-PRACTICE

Many American business leaders are rushing to adopt reengineering today. Both large and small companies have been able to understand, afford, and apply reengineering.

Are You a Candidate?

All business enterprises could adopt reengineering. However, some businesses will benefit from reengineering more than others. Unfortunately, many companies stay in denial and wait until they are "forced to change" their business approach. If you have waited too long and your business is just a step ahead of your creditors, you may not have anything to lose by applying this approach for your last-chance survival effort. Your only choice may be to overhaul your entire operation or to close your doors. The principal problem with waiting is that you may not have enough time to obtain successful outcomes from reengineering.

The second type of business enterprise that tries to adopt reengineering are those from the "me-too" management school. They are the short-lived managers who jump from one new management tool to another, the supporters of the "fad-of-the-month" organizational improvements. The problem here is that these managers do not understand the difficulty in changing their business process and culture. This type of manager is not ready to make the personnel commitment, nor assure the financial support necessary to give reengineering a chance to work.

The enterprise that will profit most from reengineering is the well-managed business that may already be a leader in its niche market. This type of business may recognize the potential of reengineering, and believe that its adoption will give it an additional competitive advantage in the marketplace in which it is already perceived as a leader.

The Role of Technology and People

As we have stated, reengineering is a people- and process-focused approach rather than a technology-focused effort.[2] The development of new state-of-the-art communication, interface, or "smart" tools will eventually be useful. But, today, we can take advantage of all the potential of reengineering by understanding and changing our processes, and by opening the communications between business functions by empowering our people to work as part of multifunctional teams.

Reengineering demands a high degree of teamwork, and this worker and co-worker involvement and peer pressure should improve overall performance and customer satisfaction.

There will be fewer workers; they will be more highly skilled, multidisciplined, and might well have the overall background of our present-day technical specialists or engineers, rather than the typical worker we see today.

This new breed of skilled worker will be able to produce products and services cheaper, better, and faster than we thought possible. Clearly, you must come to understand and support the needs of this new worker for your business to survive and prosper.

In the future, more prestigious positions in the management of your business may be filled by persons with well-rounded technical skills, as well as demonstrated people-management skills. They will have arrived at this leadership position from a series of previous assignments, including product engineering and manufacturing, production support, and quality management. Coupled with these technical skills, he or she will have been in positions requiring interaction with people, superiors, peers, and subordinate co-workers; positions that were successful because of the interactions of, and with, people.

Market demand for reengineering savvy executives, product creators, and production and process analysts will increase on a nation-wide basis.

Clearly, there will be a tremendous impact as our workforce undergoes the wrenching changes (downsizing, radical changes, and innovative product development) that will be required to restructure our new, more competitive business base. We have seen many smaller management system revolutions and their impact on the workforce, which then impacts the overall fabric of the society it supports.

Management will be challenged on all fronts if they are to successfully implement reengineering. To survive the process, managers will have to tune into and embrace change and recognize that it is not a threat, but an opportunity to achieve that elusive edge on your competitor. He or she will buy time to remain a leader in his product or service line; time to plan more change, always anticipating change and keeping ahead of what's happening with your competitors.

CHAPTER 9

Obliterate, Then Automate

One of the fundamental concerns in American business today is that we must improve our productivity in every aspect of our enterprise by providing new products and services cheaper, better, and faster than our competitors. This chapter focuses on productivity improvement; enhancement of your operations by simplifying overall processes by concentrating on system integration. Once elimination of unneeded processes has been completed, it would then be time to apply automation.

We need to obliterate old thinking, old processes, and old management concepts before we embark on automating our processes. You need to eliminate business units, product lines, downsize the overall operation by reengineering your processes, then apply systems thinking to further integrate your business operations. Only then should you embark on automating the remaining administrative and production operations.

IMPROVE YOUR PRODUCTIVITY

American businesses are slowly improving their productivity, as shown in figure 9.1. For manufacturing, this productivity growth has been less than 3 percent, with even less productivity improvement in the service sector. In order to improve our competitive position, each business leader has to look again at how they are using their total resources, and find ways to be more efficient. The process elimination, downsizing, and reengineering actions described in this book can help you improve your productivity.

By definition, productivity is a measure of useful output that results from a given set of inputs. The basic inputs include the cost of labor, capital invested in both R&D and fixed assets, raw materials, components, energy, administration, marketing and distribution. In highly automated operations, labor, for

Figure 9.1   Average Annual Productivity Growth

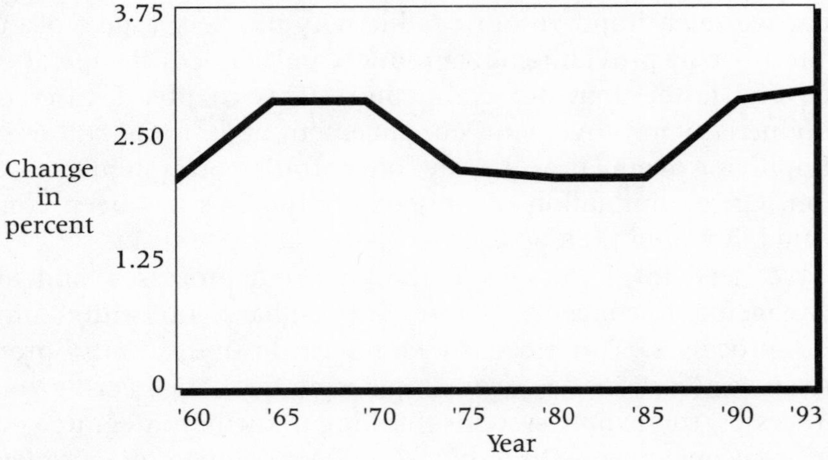

SOURCE: *Business Week* and U.S. Department of Commerce.

example, is not a significant cost, but in many service operations, it is.

Once you have reexamined your business processes, then look at using technology and automation of the remaining processes as a tool to increase your productivity. Figure 9.2 illustrates the direct effect that increased productivity can have on your bottom line.

America businesses are in a unique period of productivity enhancement, resulting from the major increases in productivity now possible for the first time through use of cost-effective computer information systems, office automation, automated manufacturing systems (such as advanced robotics, computer-aided engineering, computer-aided design and manufacturing), and

Figure 9.2   Productivity Improvement Drivers

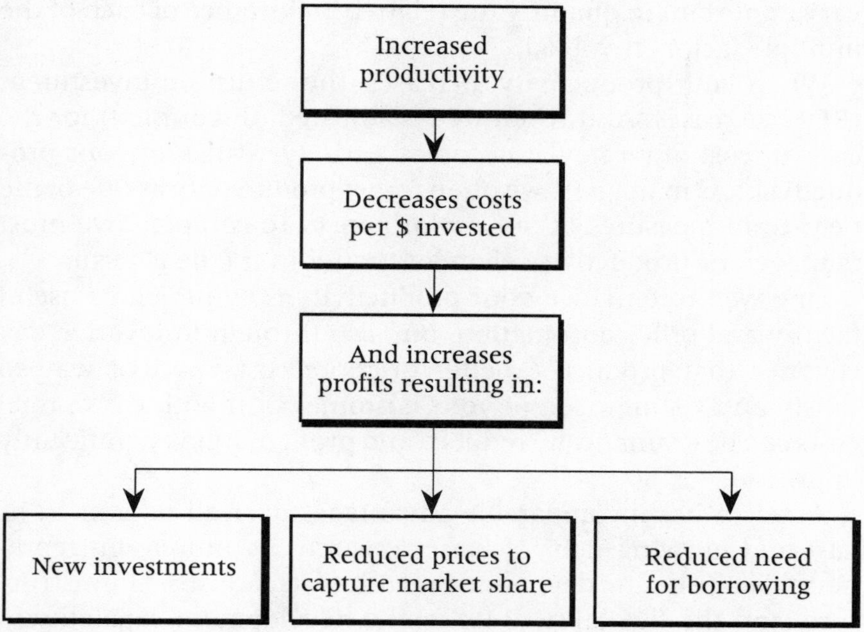

sophisticated process-oriented software. No previous period in history has had access to such a powerful array of new productivity-enhancing technologies.

According to E. Denison of the Brookings Institute, there are several key aspects that constitute productivity. Each of these elements is a target for you to improve your performance.

ELEMENT	PERCENT
Technology	38.1
Capital	25.4
Labor quality	14.3
Economies of scale	12.7
Resource allocation	9.5

Therefore, in measuring and improving your productivity, it is very important to quantify the relative importance of each of the multiple factors involved.

When your productivity increases, the return on investment (ROI) increases. And when ROI is adjusted (discounted) for the current cost of money, it becomes a true yardstick of your productivity. As managers, we often forget productivity as one of the near-term measures of our performance. To compete, we must manage our productivity elements better in the near-term.

One way to enhance your productivity is by judicious use of factory and office automation, but also through innovative discoveries that produce a better or more cost-effective way to satisfy an existing need of your customer's. In both cases, total costs can be dramatically reduced and profit margins significantly improved.

America has incomparable advantages over all nations in its vast and growing pool of basic research, its unique entrepreneurial culture, the depth and breadth of its industrial infrastructure, and the flexibility of its capital development capability in the world's largest market. But if we are to maintain the world commerce leadership position we enjoy, the climate for better productivity through technology innovation must be further enhanced.

APPLY TECHNOLOGY TO IMPROVE PRODUCTIVITY

Technology innovation is one of your keys to increased productivity and competitiveness in world markets that will depend upon continually increasing your productivity.

Innovative technology in products and processes has been the source of our economic well-being. The Japanese, for example, recognized this strength, and copied our technology, applied engineering, and management skills in a favorable economic climate, and made heavy capital investment in their plants and people; that resulted in their taking away significant markets, such as television, VCRs, and automobiles, from American business. To maintain your competitive position, you will need to apply or develop innovative technologies and apply heavy doses of well-placed capital to remain competitive.

Top management must accept the role of champion for support of the acquisition, use, or new development of technologies—where they will really improve your productivity; and commit their businesses to the application and use of cost-effective state-of-the-practice technology and automation.

OPPORTUNITY FOR SYSTEMS INTEGRATION

Fuller systems integration in the factory and office automation will be essential for survival of American firms in world markets. Within a decade, viable manufacturing operations will consist of more flexible systems that can be reprogrammed continually to produce products in lot sizes of one. This flexible programming will permit the production of a large variety of competitive products. America has the advanced technology in computers, software, sensors, and materials necessary to maintain leadership in most production areas. Automated systems even have the potential for recapturing some labor-intensive businesses that have gone offshore (textiles, semiconductors, and consumer electronics).

By using system integrated automation technology, you will be able to substitute capitalization of new facilities for labor. Improvement in your application of technology will mean the ability to produce high-quality goods and services cost-effectively, and with the flexibility to respond rapidly to changing market needs. The goal in automation should be for your plant to operate with as little labor as possible to produce the specific type of product required to satisfy your customer.

Japan, which began to experience labor shortages by the end of the 1960s, has led the way toward this aim. Japanese firms have moved toward participatory management, total quality management, kaizen, and toward the use of automation to reduce their dependence on more direct labor.

Your business can benefit by looking at the approach Japan, Singapore, Germany, and other technology-driven competitors have used to improve their productivity and bottom line performance. These world-class competitors not only integrated their information and automation systems, but they also have significantly improved their management techniques, and the quality and cost-effectiveness of their production processes.

Their initial approach focused on just-in-time logistic systems, continuous process improvements, the cooperation of labor as courted by management, and appropriate technology-supported product redesign to facilitate automated manufacture; these are all techniques that you can explore in the struggle for market share, profits, and survival. System integration of product design, documentation, and advanced manufacturing systems and production should be an integral part of your reengineering efforts.

Automation plays an increasingly important role in auto-motive and precision-optics industries; and, to the extent that manufacturing is becoming increasingly automated, advanced technology is becoming the basis of high productivity in many aspects of production processes.

Full-fledged flexible manufacturing systems are still rare in American businesses. An example of a full-fledged flexible man-ufacturing system (FMS) setup is a machine tool manufacturing operation developed by the Japanese company, Mazak. The sys-tem consists of numerically controlled machine tools for machin-ing operations, automatic material handling of parts, and robotic insertion of components. For the running of this system, human labor requirements were reduced from a usual 120 persons per shift to four for each of two shifts and zero personnel for the third shift.

For American businesses to remain competitive in the world market, you will have to create an environment that will foster technological innovation and implementation.

THE BENEFITS OF AUTOMATED SYSTEMS

Delivery to your customers of a wide set of products and service choices is the trend. Flexible, technology-driven processes are allowing production and distribution of goods in lot sizes of one; and for companies like L. L. Bean, they can accept a customer's order and ship it on the same day. One Japanese automaker introduces ten to fifteen new models per year, for example, with each model offering fifteen hundred to two thousand variations, counting choices of options and paint colors.

Appropriate use of automation technology is resulting in a shortening of production cycles, a reduction of manpower, and an increase in the rate of production operations. The Tungalloy production plant, for instance, after implementation of auto-mated systems, has sixteen workers compared with the seventy previously required, a production cycle of four days versus nineteen days, and a rate of operation increased from 20 percent to 70 percent. Individual machine tools have been reduced from fifty to six, and the floor space required from 1,480 square feet to 350 square feet. Processing costs have been cut in half.

Similarly, automated system integration has resulted in the reduction of the workforce at the Brother Industries plant from 250 to 12, under a twenty-four-hour-a-day operation. It has also reduced machine tools from forty-two to twenty-five and labor staff from twenty-four to two people. Processing costs were reduced 30 percent, while floor space requirements have gone up by only fifty square feet.

At Toyota Motor Corporation, computer-aided information automation technology was introduced at their factory for engine production, while CAD/CAM terminals have increased from 90 to 250. Many are in use in precision machinery and metal molds areas in which model changes are frequent.

Major Japanese companies such as Fanuc, Matsushita Electric, Toshiba, and Yasukawa Electric, which are building new "greenfield" factories and enlarging already-existing production facilities, are already involved in state-of-the-art factory automation.

Most of the examples of expanded use of automation technology is tied to the early use of appropriate technology in the auto industry and consumer electronics business. Office and business process capital investment in new technology and automation has lagged behind. Since the labor content of many manufacturing jobs has already been reduced to minimal levels, managers are now looking at how the same approaches at using computers, systems analysis, process simplification and integration, and investment in work-flow technology can improve the administrative support and distribution system costs in business overhead areas. Part of the downsizing and reengineering efforts greatest benefits come from flattening organizational structures, reducing the size of corporate staff and administrative jobs. But once this is done on the first major round of changes, many companies find that they have to invest in computer information systems and productivity-focused automation to fully support their leaner staff in performing their work.

IMPACT ON PEOPLE AND JOBS

All the new technology will be for naught if we are not able to create a more dedicated and motivated workforce team to satisfy our customers' needs. This will require a change in the way we have produced goods over hundreds of years. For as long as man has relied on the factory concept, he has always worked to reduce the cost of human labor and the support systems that keep it going.

This desire to maximize profit has been offset by government and union demands for social changes, including more worker benefits such as health care and occupational safety improvements. In order to survive in certain markets, American business is being forced to reengineer and adopt a new view of the value of "process change"; and to depend on a new form of labor: the skilled and semiskilled employee who can understand, operate, and repair the complex technology in place in your business. This employee is a new quantity to most "old time" managers. In demand, the new worker cannot be handled like the more abundant unskilled production worker. Also, because the new equipment operated and maintained by these workers produces materials more efficiently and at a much faster rate, failures and shutdowns affect production rates very quickly and are therefore more serious. Clearly, management must come to grips with this new technology worker.

Naturally, the transition to the "reengineered enterprise" will have its effect on employment patterns. Although operational layers of supervision are reduced drastically, even unmanned production requires workers, most in management and information system positions. As automation progresses, jobs will be lost.

There will be a shift in some jobs from one sector of the economy to another. The proportion of the workforce involved in manufacturing production will continue to decline; the proportion involved in service occupations will increase. Even without automation, manufacturing jobs will decrease, as U.S. firms either move factories elsewhere (Mexico, and the Pacific Rim) or go out of business due to increasing competitive pressure; this is clearly seen today in the clothing, semiconductor, and consumer electronics business areas.

The need for white-collar workers will be reduced significantly due to the implementation of automation technology in the office administration areas. For example, new low-cost speech recognition technology will allow you to dictate a letter to your computer and have it immediately typed and printed out or distributed over the "information highway"—this one technology tool alone will obsolete many secretary/typists and data entry employees. Other jobs will be reduced for cost savings. Scheduling and planning will be performed by expert systems, and performance measurement will be tracked in real time.

By the year 2000, only 10 percent of the labor force will be engaged in manufacturing, as opposed to the 22 percent of 1980. Older, unskilled, displaced workers will find it difficult to find employment without significant growth in our economy.

Automation will have a very large effect on senior and middle managers and the corporate structure of most companies. Both fewer supervisors and fewer workers will be needed. More workers will be supervised by each manager. The traditional ratio (span of control) of one supervisor for five employees is being changed dramatically in some businesses to one supervisor for fifteen to twenty employees. The number of experienced managers will decline, with top management being closer to your business operations.

Technology and automation will adversely affect many of your employees, as summarized below:

- Worker displacement will affect the total organization population, but will be especially heavy in the areas of manufacturing (painting, welding, flame cutting, machinist and machine operation, and component assembly) and office and administration (clerical, secretarial, administrative management, and staff specialists) employees. Displacements will double between 1990 and 1995.

- Man-hours will be reduced heavily in those businesses dealing in aerospace, machinery, automotive, fabricated metal products, primary metals, and consumer nondurable goods.

- Fifty percent of the technical personnel your business will need will come from colleges and universities, with most of the remainder being retrained in-house personnel, primarily engineers and technicians rather than other workers.

Such a management shift will cause a rethinking of traditional operational structures. Enhanced communication possibilities mean that executives may not be housed in one major central headquarters facility. Also, the executive of the future will be better educated to deal with automation, technology, and development of computer information systems and will be able to make better judgments based on such information.

Your employees have always known of better ways to do things. Suggestion programs abound in most organizations, from administration, engineering, manufacturing, to customer support. No one person or group operation is so efficient that it can't be improved by another approach, idea, or process improvement. Never is it more important to explore new ideas than when your product or services suffer from poor quality.

It appears that Japanese workers, like their American counterparts, are a source of valuable suggestions. Japanese management recognized this as a very inexpensive way to add value to a product or service, and at the same time give the employee a greater sense of value and belonging. Automation is not always the most cost-effective course of action to turn around your business. In some cases, focusing on employee involvement, and changing your business processes, can provide significant near-term improvements to your business.

In the future, many of the more prestigious management positions will be taken by persons with well-rounded technical skills, as well as by those with demonstrated change management skills. They would have arrived at this position from a series of previous assignments, including product engineering and manufacturing, production support, quality control, and customer service. Such managers will have been in positions requiring interaction with superiors, peers, and subordinate co-workers.

Another trend in evidence today is in the recruitment of managers and engineers with advanced degrees. For many years, the employers for such people were mainly the universities and the military-industrial complex, a pattern that is changing, as graduate programs are modified or replaced to keep up with the rapid pace of technology. Fearing obsolescence, many advanced-degree engineers and scientists have chosen to become part of the technology push in the outside world rather than be pulled by the technology in the university. Indications are that these graduate-level personnel are being employed at an ever-increasing rate in the business community rather than in the defense industries.

Considering the approximately 370,000 Ph.D. engineers and scientists that are in the workforce:

❑ The sharpest increases for employment of Ph.D. holders occurred in business application areas such as sales, production, quality, and consulting.

❑ Business and industry-related employment accounts for 21 percent of the work of Ph.D.'s.

Market demand for younger high-technology, change-oriented executives is on the rise nationwide. Business operations, information systems, and general management executives will still be in demand.

The trends now in motion to draw the technically talented individuals into business will be a most rewarding experience for those fortunate to be in the position to benefit from the push to apply systems thinking, advanced technology, and related automation.

We are a nation characterized by progress. Whenever we stop to enjoy that success derived from being an innovator, we become fair prey to our competitors, who are moving up that same technological curve. The advantage that we enjoy is one of time—the time it takes for someone else to reach our level of development. For a while, it will then be possible to enjoy the prosperity; but if we think that it will last indefinitely without further improvement, we become a statistic or a footnote in the "also ran" book of competitors.

Even though significant change is at hand, there is still time for you to ensure a reasonable business transition from the present to the near future, by adopting a technology-supported process improvement approach for your business today.

Clearly, there will be tremendous impact as our workforce undergoes the wrenching changes that will be required to restructure and reengineer our products and processes to assure the survival of our businesses.

CHAPTER 10

Empower Your Team

As your work becomes increasingly sophisticated, and as the demands for your business to improve performance and adapt to ever-faster changing conditions accelerate, there is an ever-greater need for your employees to operate in a cooperative and synergistic fashion as part of a team. And managers in turn are finding new ways to develop and empower their teams to provide higher performance.

Team building is one of the most common and effective near-term strategies that business leaders can use to increase their capacity to perform. This chapter defines team building (both process improvement and multifunctional teams), describes when team building is an appropriate activity, presents clearly the overall team-building process, and discusses the impact of team building on your business.

However, before addressing team building, it is important to understand what makes for a high performance team.

WHAT IS A HIGH PERFORMANCE TEAM?

Almost everyone has experience either being on a high performance team or watching one in action. While sports teams, such as football and soccer, are an obvious arena to look for high performance teams, they also exist in business organizations, churches, community groups—even in families. And while there may be tremendous differences in their task, structure, and makeup, high performance teams share several key characteristics:

- The team members share a common vision for what they are committed to achieve, based on a clear perception of the value that the team can provide for its customers.

- The team has a well-developed strategy for realizing its vision.

- Team members collectively possess the necessary skills and knowledge, and they share responsibility for fulfillment of your survival strategy.

- The procedures, systems, and methods are appropriate, clear, efficient, and adaptable as needed.

- Relations among team members are open, challenging, and supportive.

- There is active engagement between process improvement teams, multifunctional teams, and other individuals, and business organizations to ensure that the team remains vital, adaptable, and relevant to the task at hand.

Virtually every high performance team possesses these characteristics to some degree; it is the objective of team building to help your teams more fully display these winning characteristics.

Team building is a structured process that is based on organizational development concepts. As most commonly practiced, team building is often based around one or more key improvement activities, process improvements, or team communication building sessions.

During the team-building phase, team members learn how to work together and resolve operational problems. The team identifies specific areas that are either inhibiting their performance or could be strengthened, and comes to agreement on ways to reach a higher state of performance. In the General Electric model, team members come together to describe and recommend immediate action for their managers to resolve. General Electric calls their process "work-out," and it was designed to improve their team communication and performance. It is a proven process for near-term breakdown of organizational stovepipe boundaries in their business. You can use these concepts today in your own business.

During the team-building process, teams focus on a variety of business change issues. In addition, the team also periodically steps back to reflect on its own processes of communication, problem solving, and decision making during the team-building effort. In this way, team building is both a planning and problem-solving effort that is used to better understand your team's own strengths and weaknesses.

CREATING MULTIFUNCTIONAL TEAMS

Survival goes beyond management leadership and decision making—it includes defining the problem, generating alternative solutions, evaluating alternatives, selecting alternatives, and implementing the solution. The problems are multileveled, multidimensional, and multidisciplinary—all of the information required to make sound decisions to solve your near-term problems may not be available, and the available information may be based on "seat-of-the-pants" judgment and your own experience. Your business survival depends on complex human interaction among your co-workers with diverse backgrounds and from various disciplines.

The success of each turnaround effort depends on the ability of your team members to work together; thus, team satisfaction with the change process and the resulting product and process definition is important. Achieving consensus among members of your team means arriving at a product and process definition that your co-workers can agree upon. Each member may not think the new approach is the absolute best attainable, but in agreeing to a particular process, each member must believe that it is a "good" process and that all essential elements have been included. Having all members satisfied with the change process ensures ownership and responsibility among team members. Once consensus is achieved among the team members, it is essential that buy-in is achieved from management. The preferred method is by maintaining open communication during the process to prevent management objections during the implementation phase.

The multifunctional nature of the teams complicates the group dynamics because of technical language barriers, perceptions of unequal status, and general cultural barriers to teamwork. Some of the disconnects include the following.

- Rigid, functionally dominated organizational structures exist that resist any change.

- Everyone's functional organization base becomes the center of their universe.

- Process analysts, software and hardware engineers see themselves as creative individuals who do not want that creativity restricted by having to accommodate indirect functional or process concerns.

- Manufacturing is concerned about satisfying customers' current orders and maintaining their production flow stability.

Management must overcome these obstacles if your process reengineering team is to work effectively.

Some of the various organizational and management strategies business is practicing to fully utilize multifunctional teams
are summarized below.[1]

Team of Teams

A general rule for effective group interaction is that the team's
size should not exceed eight to twelve members. However, the
development of a complex product can require hundreds of
people from various functional groups in an organization. The
complete team performs, therefore, as a team of teams. The use
of the team here has more to do with a way of thinking about
process problem solution than the size of the group. The typical
process improvement team consists of co-workers who operate
from a shared agenda and a common view of their assignment.

A team of teams is usually a hierarchy of teams that follows the
decomposition of the process down to the smallest element of
action. The term "hierarchy" here does not apply to the status of
the teams or team members but rather to the relationships
among the teams and how these relationships correspond to
process elimination, simplification, or other process changes.
Communication can be maintained among teams by placing a
member (usually the team leader) from a lower-level team on a
team at the next highest level. The high-level team defines the
strategic or system integration of the results of the other teams.

There is usually at least one team for each node of product or
process development. If the product and process definition for
the next level requires more than a dozen people, the teams are
further divided by discipline or technology. The decomposition
occurs until the subsystems can be defined by a manageable
group (eight to twelve people). The theory behind organizing the
teams along discipline or technology lines either within the
product or process element is that grouping people by functional
or technical discipline is a way to break the language barrier so
often encountered when people who have traditionally per-

formed different functions try to communicate. Most members of the same discipline speak the same language, regardless of their function. For example, mechanical engineers, whether from the engineering, manufacturing, or support group, will understand most of one another's technical terms because of common education. Financial officers, human resource specialists, and different technical and information specialists have similar common vocabularies and viewpoints and usually are able to talk with one another. The problem is to get multifunctional groups to communicate to help solve your problems.

Team Management

Successful management of a team relies on the same types of effective policies and actions to make management of any business organization successful. A team is, after all, somewhat like a small organization. Following are some of the activities that characterize effective team management:

❏ Effective structuring of the team's organizational design (roles, responsibilities, authority, and accountability).

❏ Preparation of a clear, concise team charter, task or mission statement.

❏ Identification of the goals or milestones that the team is expected to accomplish in working toward its mission or purpose.

❏ Delineation of the strategy of the team to include major policies, programs, procedures, plans, and budgets.

Regardless of the type of organizational structure selected for team formation, each team needs to have a sponsor. The team sponsor can be either a person or a team of people at the management or supervisor level, such as a designated vice president or the reengineering champion. For projects that involve more than one company, the multicorporation team should involve individuals from all the companies involved. This oversight management team is the sponsor of all teams involved in improving your processes.

The team sponsor supports the team's activities, secures resources, and opens communication lines between the team and the rest of the department, the division, and the organization. Sponsors should possess a personal stake in the success of your effort, control over the resources needed to launch and sustain the effort, and the authority to empower the team and remove any roadblocks to its success. The sponsor can do a lot to help the team overcome inefficient processes embedded in the culture of the organization. For example, a reason might once have existed for extensive paperwork between people on a project team. Many decisions can be reached through the face-to-face interaction of the team members. The extensive paperwork may no longer be needed, but not only is it required by the organization's business practices, it also is instilled in the cultural practices of the team members. The sponsor should help remove these inefficiencies in existing "cultural" processes.

Team Membership

Much of the success of a team is determined by the choice of team members. Teams may involve both blue-collar and white-collar, union and nonunion workers. Achieving the required level of teamwork requires a structured process and competent people with specific expertise and understanding of the customer's needs, product or process requirements, technology base, information, materials, production capabilities, and administrative support capabilities.

The formation of your team carries with it no guarantee that team members will talk with one another. The team must include the right leader, as well as the right team members. Peter

Scholtes has defined in *The Team Handbook*, that team leaders are the members responsible for managing the team. His or her duties include:

- Calling and directing all team meetings.
- Orchestrating all team activities.
- Overseeing the preparation of reports, presentations, meeting agendas, and minutes.
- Handling or assigning administrative detail.
- Ensuring timely analysis and resolution of technical decisions.

Team leaders can be responsible for specific processes under examination. The team leader is a full-fledged team member who shares the responsibilities of attending meetings, carrying out assignments between meetings, and generally sharing in the team's work. In addition, the team leader is the point of communication between the team and the rest of the organization, specifically the team sponsor.

One organizational element that has proven successful for many survival teams is collocation of the team members. The benefits of collocation include:

- Fostering of informal communication among strategic and operational team members.
- Reduction in functional allegiance and adversarial relationships.
- Cultivation of flexible relationships, an appreciation of each other's concerns.
- Creation of a participative atmosphere.

Often the collocated members change over the duration of the project. As its work progresses, the team may recruit new people to solve specific problems. Originally, all the team members may be collocated, but as the size of the team grows, collocation of all the new members may not be possible. At some point, teams may become so large that many of the benefits of collocation are no longer realized—a person is limited in how many other people he or she can informally communicate with within any given time period.

HOW TO RUN BETTER TEAM MEETINGS

Effective team meetings are among the best opportunities to enhance the team-building process and make progress toward accomplishing your goals. To enhance the effectiveness of team meetings, the following procedures are often recommended:

- ❑ Limit the duration of team meetings.
- ❑ Use agendas and record minutes.
- ❑ Do not end a meeting without specifying and assigning the action items.
- ❑ Do not let more than two weeks elapse between meetings.

Discipline is an important element contributing to the success of your team meetings and, thus, to the team itself. You should emphasize that each meeting must be held for a specific purpose and not merely just to have a meeting. Meeting activities should be strictly limited to the agenda items, and all of these activities have a deliverable focus. In addition, what is said is recorded. This level of meeting documentation should be created for all of the meetings as well as the management reviews.

HOW TO START A TEAM

Creating a team (process improvement team or multifunctional team) is an appropriate management tool under any one of four different scenarios.

1. A new product or process improvement has been authorized and a new team has been formed to address the specific problem, and the team needs to create a clear working arrangement for itself.

2. The improvement activities for your business have experienced considerable difficulty or distress, either in performance or communication of your process change needs.

3. The process improvement activities have been narrowly focused and a more diverse set of corporate functional process areas needs to be brought together in multifunctional teams to resolve "bigger" problems, to obtain higher productivity or significant new levels of change to assure your survival.

4. Your teams are functioning effectively, but you need to reassess your performance periodically, and resolve any complex issues before they become serious or chronic, and identify new opportunities for change, growth, and development.

As the pace of change increases and as work demands become more complex, there is an ever-greater need for work groups to operate effectively as teams. And as managers look for new ways to start their teams off in an effective way, they often consider developing teams.

If you are such a manager, the following points have been prepared to help you understand the overall objectives of starting a team, when it might be appropriate, what conditions must be met in order for your effort to succeed, how the process works, and what its likely impact would be. Guidance is also provided for how to proceed, should you decide that a team approach makes sense for your business.

Effective teams, regardless of where they exist, share certain characteristics:

- Team members have a clear commitment to the team's goals, and find that their individual goals are highly compatible with the team's.

- Team members' roles and responsibilities are clear, including their relationships with one another.

- The established procedures for functioning are clear, appropriate, efficient, and open to modification as needs arise.

- Relationships within the team are characterized by open communications, direct messages, high conflict over substance and low conflict over interpersonal issues, and mutual trust and dependability.

While it may be idealistic to expect a team to possess fully each of these characteristics, it is the objective of the team leader to start groups in that direction.

In the past ten to fifteen years, a great deal has been learned about how to develop teams to focus on near-term achievement of your business goals. Teams are usually newly formed work groups, be they process improvement teams, multifunctional teams, product development groups, task forces, ongoing work teams, or any of these that have substantially new members or new mission focus.

Your new team start-up orientation should be done as quickly after the team has been created as possible, and before any major efforts are made toward organizing or moving toward mission accomplishment. The team orientation can be done in a retreat format, away from the work site, to provide uninterrupted time for team members to get acquainted and to focus on the team building and empowerment process. Often a facilitator is hired from outside the group to help plan the session and to help the team leader conduct it.

The creation of a team may be appropriate under several scenarios, including:

1. The team is relatively new and wants to establish beneficial patterns of performance from the outset.

2. The team members are coming together from different organizations and want to clarify their values, perceptions, and team mission.

3. The team has been established to operate effectively together, but believes that an even greater level of performance or satisfaction is possible.

In general, new teams will only work when there is a perceived need from within the team, as opposed to being seen as a "good thing to do," the latest fad, or because someone else thinks it should be done. In particular, it is critical that the team leader be fully committed to the process.

There are basically five conditions for a successful team effort:

1. The perceived need on the part of the team leader and, hopefully, the team for such an effort.

2. The involvement of a qualified facilitator, either internal or external to your business.

3. The commitment of time: for the team leader and the facilitator to plan the overall start-up process; structure the session; and for all members to participate in a retreat. (A new team start-up session requires two and a half to four days in most instances.)

4. A commitment on the team leader's part to the philosophy and practices of teamwork, especially around open communications, and the participation of team members in decision making.

5. Commitment of the team to engage actively in the team process, including implementing decisions made at the sessions and additional activities as needed.

The financial costs of a new team start-up session could vary, depending on whether or not an external facilitator is engaged. In addition, a suitable off-site facility is required in order to provide an environment conducive to a relaxed sharing of thoughts and feelings on topics that are potentially controversial or volatile in terms of the potential changes needed to help your business change.

THE TEAM DEVELOPMENT PROCESS

There is a basic sequence of tasks that comprises most new team start-up efforts, as shown in figure 10.1, consisting of tasks that occur prior to the team session, during the session, and after the session.

Before Session

1. Facilitator and team leader clarify objectives and plan the overall process.

2. Facilitator meets with entire team to discuss objectives, explain the overall process, and identify any particular areas that team members would like the facilitator to focus on during the team session.

Figure 10.1   New Team Start-up Process

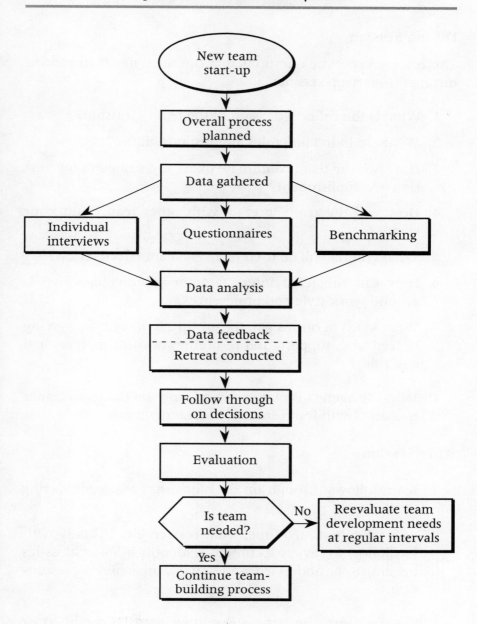

During Session

There are seven basic questions that the team needs to address during the start-up session:

1. What is the collective vision of the team's mission?

2. What are individual roles and responsibilities?

3. How will the team coordinate plans and strategies for mission accomplishment?

4. How will the team interact with other teams and your clients?

5. What criteria will be used to assess team effectiveness?

6. How can the team interact to meet individuals' needs around work style and preferences?

7. What kinds of norms will the group adopt regarding giving of feedback, support, and resolution of conflicts (personal and role)?

Usually, the agenda is planned in advance by the team leader and facilitator, with input from the team members.

After Session

1. Team follows through on decisions that are made during session.

2. At a predetermined time, team reassembles (usually with facilitator) to review its progress, identify additional issues needing to be addressed, and to work on achieving resolution.

While these are the basic steps, they may be modified or enhanced, depending on the needs of the team or the particular style of the facilitator.

TEAM DEVELOPMENT RESULTS

At a new team's start-up session, they usually address issues that can provide the basis of a firm foundation for the future working relationships of team members. In many cases, the press of business simply prevents the kind of thorough and open communication that is possible in this kind of setting. There is often a palpable "sigh of relief" as a result of new team start-up, in that feelings and thoughts are aired, usually without the negative consequences that may have been anticipated.

In addition, a new team start-up usually results in:

❑ Norms of behavior being set or reinforced;

❑ Plans for improved communication and performance;

❑ Increased commitment to the team's goals and a team approach;

❑ Enhanced appreciation of the contributions each member makes to the team's mission.

The decisions that are made and the tone that is set in the team start-up sessions need continuing attention on the part of the entire team, especially the leader. In addition, a follow-up session is usually important for assessing the team's development and continuing the team-building process. Such a session would typically occur six to twelve months after the initial session.

What has been provided here is a variety of factors to consider when weighing the potential value of teams. This is likely to be a valuable option if there is a strong desire for enhancing your business effectiveness and when the necessary conditions exist, including the willingness to commit the financial and staff resources to make this process work.

Team building usually results in a team's enhanced functioning in a high performance mode. This happens as a result of learning more about what it means to operate as a team, addressing issues that are getting in the way of your team's effectiveness, and learning new techniques and principles that foster cooperative and synergistic teamwork.

Some teams have been involved in team building as a single and isolated event in the life of their team. When this occurs, the value of the session often drops off quickly, as the initial glow of a successful improvement effort wears off. While there may be various reasons for this, it may have to do with how realistic are the expectations about the team development process.

On one level, team building can be seen as the beginning of functioning differently, by focusing on the collective responsibility of the team's accomplishments in changing your business processes. As with any change, it is critical to allow a period of time following your team start-up for full implementation of the agreements and principles developed during the process improvement sessions. This period of implementation should then be followed with another session (often briefer than the first) to review progress, and make corrections, adjustments, or enhancements.

Therefore, team building is best seen not as a one-time event, but rather as an ongoing process of team growth and renewal.

TEAM EFFECTIVENESS ANALYSIS

The work of your business is frequently accomplished in temporary or permanent work groups. Organization and team effectiveness depends on a process of developing and evaluating functional work units. To remain viable, an organization needs the creativity, insights, knowledge, and experience of every team member for the development of functional plans, procedures, action plans, and even the evaluation of its own work.

It is an unwise assumption to conclude that effective teamwork will happen as a natural consequence of bringing together a group of individuals and giving that group a common task. Good teamwork can be enhanced by an organized learning process focusing on analyzing several factors required for effective teamwork.

Personal growth in leadership and team membership calls for increasing awareness and knowledge of the complex causes of group and organizational behavior, more sensitivity to the feelings and needs of others, and expanding skill in working effectively with others in team situations.

Teamwork, like most relationships, requires commitment, skills and attention to the task at hand. In order to help assess the implementation of your team-building process, the following three-part self-assessment[2] is provided.

Research and experience have indicated that eight key teamwork factors are essential to the relationships of a group. Prior to turning to part II, please list some basic information about the team you will be analyzing as delineated in part I.

Part I

BACKGROUND

1. Team you will analyze: _____

2. Size of team: _____

3. How long has the team been in existence? _____

4. How long have you been a member of the team? _____

5. Are you the team leader? _____

6. If so, how long? _____

7. How would you rate the present level of teamwork in your group?

Excellent _____ Very good _____ Fair _____ Poor _____

8. How important is it to you to see teamwork improve in this group?

_____   _____   _____   _____
Very   Important   Somewhat   Unimportant
important   important

Part II

A YARDSTICK FOR MEASURING
TEAM PERFORMANCE

As a team begins its life, and at several points during its growth, the team leader and members should reflect on the following factors and spend some time sharing the data collected. Through rating each factor, it is possible to get a general picture of the perceptions that various members have about the team and how it is developing. It is also possible to identify areas in which there may be some difficulties blocking progress. Each person should rate the group chosen on the following factors.

A. *Goal clarity* (within the total organization, for the task at hand, and for the individuals involved; short- and long-range goals; individual commitment as well as understanding).

1	2	3	4	5
No apparent goals	Goal confusion	Average goal clarity	Goals mostly clear	Goals very clear

B. *Trust and openness* (that encourage open and frank communication resulting in high tolerance for differences of opinions and personalities).

1	2	3	4	5
No trust and no openness	Little trust and openness	Average trust and openness	Considerable trust and openness	Remarkable trust and openness

C. *Empathy among members* (a mature level of respect, not sympathy, does not mean it is necessary to like someone to work with that person).

1	2	3	4	5
No empathy	Little empathy	Average empathy	Considerable empathy	Remarkable empathy

D. Balance between group task and maintenance needs (task needs—getting the job done and content covered; and maintenance needs—keeping the team process running well).

1	2	3	4	5
No balance	Little balance	Average balance	A good balance	Excellent balance

E. Leadership needs (common understanding, acceptance and performance of leadership; and determining what kind of leadership [from one person to shared] is needed).

1	2	3	4	5
Leadership needs not met	Some leadership needs met	Average meeting of leadership needs	Good meeting of leadership needs	Excellent meeting of leadership needs

F. Decision making (initiation and implementation; consideration of minority viewpoints; securing each members' commitment).

1	2	3	4	5
Unable to reach decisions	Inadequate decision making	Average decision making	Good decision making	Excellent decision making

G. Use of group resources (particularly for complex tasks and problem solving requiring the resources of more than one person; searching for and using relevant knowledge and skills).

1	2	3	4	5
Group resources not used	Group resources poorly used	Average use of group resources	Group resources well used	Group resources fully and effectively used

H. Sense of belonging (not blind loyalty, but wanting to work with others to accomplish goals; appropriate cohesion among members).

1	2	3	4	5
No sense of belonging	Some sense of belonging	Average sense of belonging	Good sense of belonging	Strong sense of belonging

Part III

EXAMINING YOUR RATINGS

1. On what three factors in part II did you rate your team the *highest*?

Factor ranked #1 _____

Factor ranked #2 _____

Factor ranked #3 _____

What evidence can you cite to justify these three ratings?

Factor #1 _____

Factor #2 _____

Factor #3 _____

2. On what three items in part II did you rate your group the *lowest*?

Factor #1 _____

Factor #2 _____

Factor #3 _____

What evidence can you cite to justify your ratings?

Factor Ranked #1 _____

Factor Ranked #2 _____

Factor Ranked #3 _____

3. How do you predict that your ratings will compare with others in the team? Which might be lower or higher? Why?

Part IV

TABULATION DIRECTIONS

In your team, share the ratings of each member of the team and put these individual ratings on a chart in front of your team for discussion purpose. Now that you have received both your own rating of the team and those of other members of the team, work with the team in planning the discussion and analysis of the results.

Possible Discussion Questions

1. What are the causes underlying those factors receiving the lowest scores among the members of your team?

2. What are the causes underlying those factors receiving the highest scores among the members of your team?

3. Why was there such a wide difference of opinion on certain factors?

Part V

STEPS IN IMPROVING TEAMWORK

1. Some of the action steps that I as a member of the team can take to improve are: _____

_____

2. Some of the action steps that the team might take to improve our teamwork are: _____

_____

_____

3. Some of the action steps that the team leader might take to improve our teamwork are: _____

_____

The review and implementation of these action steps can be determined by your team members now, and by repeating the process at a later time as part of your continuing process of team building.

CHAPTER 11

Pay for Skills and Performance

Revolutionary changes are coming to some businesses in terms of "broad banding" (reducing the number of pay categories), to pay-for-performance, and pay-for-knowledge that is directly applied to a job.

Each of these techniques can improve your management flexibility and productivity if properly applied. This chapter provides an overview of each of these pay process change approaches.

BROAD BANDING INCREASES FLEXIBILITY

Over the past couple of years, the concept of "broad banding"— that is, collapsing the number of salary ranges within a traditional salary structure into a few broad bands—has drawn considerable attention. And while the number of companies that have gone to broad banding is increasing, it is not necessarily the answer for everyone. The following material on broad banding is adapted with the permission of Hewitt Associates LLC, one of the leaders in the design and implementation of broad-banding systems.[1]

You need to be sure that you are adopting broad banding for the right reasons. It is not a solution to a compensation problem, but an approach to compensation that responds to very specific organization and workforce needs. Employers need to be aware that broad banding can raise a host of complex compensation issues—both philosophical and administrative—that must be addressed.

What Is Broad Banding?

Broad banding is the use of salary structures with significantly fewer grades (or bands) and much wider ranges than what has been considered the "norm" in the past. Jobs that previously were covered by as many as four or five grades typically are consolidated into a single band with one minimum and one maximum. Salary range midpoints usually are not used because a band encompasses so many jobs of differing values.

This type of structure offers greater flexibility to employers who need to define job responsibilities more broadly. It also facilitates career growth and development for employees without many of the administrative burdens traditionally associated with promotions, transfers, and the like.

Figure 11.1 illustrates how you might convert four salary grades into one band. As indicated in the example, range spreads for the bands are usually about twice as wide as conventional salary range spreads.

When Is a Broad-Banding Approach Appropriate?

Companies that have streamlined their organization structure, and are in the process of eliminating layers of management, creating a flatter organization, will likely find value in broad

Figure 11.1   Example of Broad Banding

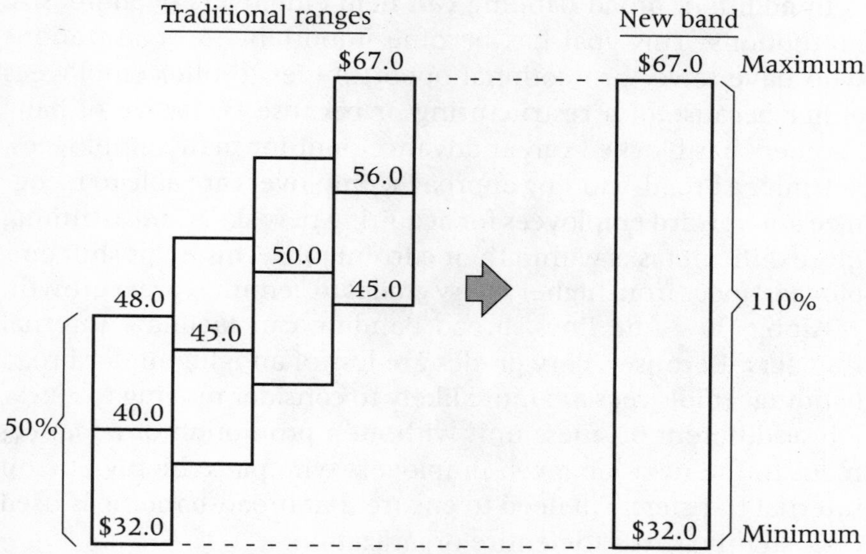

Traditional ranges

New band

$67.0 $67.0   Maximum

56.0

50.0

48.0   45.0

45.0

40.0

}110%

50%{

$32.0 $32.0 } Minimum

SOURCE: Hewitt Associates, LCC

banding. For some companies, the change in structure has been due to a merger, reorganization, reengineering, or downsizing. For others, the impetus has come from the desire to push responsibility down in the organization and foster a greater sense of teamwork. Either way, the goal usually is to increase your efficiency, flexibility, and productivity.

You may find that broad banding offers an effective way to support many of your new business goals, while minimizing the need to constantly analyze, document, and evaluate differences in job values.

For example, one of the common goals of employers in this situation is to increase workforce mobility. That is, employers want employees to become more broadly skilled so they can move from project to project or task to task with greater ease. Broad banding facilitates this flexibility by allowing an employer to add to or change the responsibilities of a job in response to organizational needs—without reevaluating or reclassifying the job.

In addition, broad banding can help employers deemphasize promotions. This goal has become important to organizations who have fewer promotional opportunities to offer employees either because of a restructuring or because the wave of baby boomers has blocked career advancement for many employees.

Under a broad-banding approach, employers are able to recognize and reward employees for acquiring new skills and assuming more difficult tasks within their current jobs. This helps shift employees' focus from higher salary grades to genuine career growth.

Along the same lines, broad banding can facilitate internal transfers. Because salary grades are less of an issue under broad banding, employees are more likely to consider moving to a new job or different business unit without a promotion or advancement to the next job level. Employers who place high value on internal transfers will need to ensure that broad-banding is used consistently across the entire organization.

Finally, broad banding allows employers to place more emphasis on individual performance because pay is no longer mechanically determined by salary ranges and rigid increase guidelines. In addition, wider salary ranges provide employers with more room to distinguish between good and mediocre performers. Accordingly, employers need to have sound performance management systems in place to ensure pay is administered appropriately.

The implications of moving to broad banding go far beyond the mechanics of design. Probably one of the most important issues you need to consider up front is whether your organization's culture and overall philosophy will support broad banding. An organization whose culture emphasizes hierarchies and places value on promotions and status will have a difficult time.

For broad banding to be successful, management and employees alike need to change the way they think about work and pay. For example, managers and their subordinates need to be comfortable with the notion that they may both fall within the same pay band. And top management needs to support the practice of making individual managers responsible for pay decisions.

Beyond the issue of culture, employers adopting broad banding need to address a number of important salary administration considerations such as:

Cost Control. Under a traditional salary structure, narrow range spreads serve as an automatic cost-control mechanism for pay. Employers need to be aware that with broad banding, there is the potential for all employees to float to the maximum—which for many jobs in the band would be much higher than market value. (Especially for employers whose payroll is 50 or 60 percent of operating expenses, small overpayment can be significant.) As such, employers adopting broad banding need to develop other cost-control strategies.

Internal Equity. Under a broad-banding approach, pay decisions become more decentralized and are less driven by strict guidelines. Employers who place a high priority on internal equity may need to develop a system for reviewing and monitoring pay decisions made by managers to ensure equity across the organization.

Relationship to Market. Without the benefit of midpoints, employers will find it more difficult to measure the value of a job relative to the marketplace. This means employers using broad banding need more (and better) market data. Moreover, employers need to share market data directly with managers responsible for making pay decisions and redefine how the data are to be used.

Job Evaluation Methodologies. Organizations using bands tend to define jobs more broadly. This, along with the fact that all jobs are slotted into one of a few bands (versus many grades), means that the role of some traditional forms of job evaluation may be reduced. Systems capable of measuring small differences in job value are no longer as critical. However, since movement from one band to the next has a dramatic impact on a job's pay range, employers need to develop a job analysis approach to control the assignment of jobs to bands.

Administrative Systems. Moving to broad banding requires employers to evaluate (and likely change) the way compensation data are stored, managed, and retrieved from existing computer systems. Existing reports often need to be redesigned and new reports and analyses need to be developed. In addition, traditional approaches to salary increases are not as relevant under broad banding, so employers typically need to develop a new set of merit increase guidelines.

Two elements critical to the successful implementation of broad banding are manager training and employee communication.

Under broad banding, the focus of pay shifts from the job to the incumbent. By necessity, this means the burden of salary administration falls on the shoulders of managers who are best able to evaluate individual performance. Employers adopting broad banding need to provide extensive training for managers—not only to educate them, but also to gain their support.

Since broad banding requires managers to interact directly with employees on compensation issues, it is imperative that they understand the rationale for the shift to broad banding and how it supports the organization's strategic direction. Just as important, training needs to stress the significance of the performance management system and provide the tools and guidelines necessary to help managers make appropriate pay decisions.

On the employee communication front, employers need to explain what broad banding is, how it works, and why the organization is adopting it. In addition, employers must reshape employee expectations about pay opportunities. For example, communication should address how broad banding affects job values and where different jobs fit into a band; highlight the stronger link between pay and individual performance; explain that not all employees will reach the maximum in their band; and note that promotions (as defined by a higher grade level) will occur less frequently.

Broad banding is not a compensation system fix. It is an approach intended to support organization change strategies. Success will require management to be open to adjusting and fine-tuning the program over time, as well as committed to ongoing training and communication.

EXPERIENCE WITH BROAD BANDING

The topic of broad bands (or career bands) is being discussed everywhere. Nevertheless, the number of companies that have implemented broad bands remains quite low. In fact, the number of companies that use them throughout their organization may be counted without the aid of calculators or computers.

We want to look beyond the theory of broad bands and provide you with data based on recent business experience with broad bands. This information is based on data from a Hewitt Associates survey and explores implementation issues that you should consider when introducing broad bands.

On the surface, many broad-band structures look alike. A single band usually spans the pay opportunity formerly covered by several separate salary ranges. Most bands have a minimum and a maximum, but no midpoint. Adjoining bands overlap, as do traditional salary ranges. Figure 11.1 shows a conversion of typical salary grades to bands.

However, not all bands are alike. Perhaps the most noteworthy difference occurs between "career bands" and what we'll call "wide salary ranges." Career bands serve primarily as a management development and communications vehicle. Their purpose may be to support a delayered environment, take attention off salary grades, and reinforce the fact that true advancement opportunities include lateral, as well as vertical, moves. As will be seen later in the discussion of specific implementation issues, merit increases, promotions, and other compensation-related practices will probably need to change in these situations.

On the other hand, with wide salary ranges, the move to bands may be based on a desire to simply expand or widen the salary ranges. The purpose may be to alleviate the "topping out" of large numbers of employees who are at, or near, the maximums of their ranges. Or it may be to simplify the administrative effort required to support the overall compensation program. Since in broad-band environments there is reduced need for job evaluation, geographic salary structures, and merit increase matrices, there are bona fide time savings in administering salaries.

The Hewitt Associates survey data indicate that over 60 percent of the participating companies that have implemented or considered bands did so in order to facilitate job transfers and lateral job mobility. Among the same group, about 30 percent implemented bands to simplify or reduce administrative effort. In fact, over twice as many companies turned to bands to support organization-wide reengineering objectives, rather than compensation-specific objectives.

Broad bands are currently used primarily for domestic employees. Of the companies that have implemented bands, over a fourth cover top executives only. Another fourth have implemented bands within specific functional groups, such as sales, manufacturing, or customer service. Only one in five use bands across all salaried employees. The remainder have implemented bands by business unit or for other employee groups.

Perhaps one of the most surprising indications from Hewitt's survey is that fully half of all companies that have implemented bands cover less than 10 percent of their employee population in the banding system.

The decision to implement bands must be made after a careful analysis of the specific objectives a company seeks to achieve. The design and administration of the bands will differ depending on the intended purpose.

The Design Process

The Hewitt Associates design process for implementing broad bands involves several important steps. The flowchart in figure 11.2 illustrates a typical design process that has been followed by several companies.

The process begins with establishing corporate or business unit objectives. Very often, the implementation of bands follows a significant organizational event, such as a merger/acquisition, reengineering, downsizing, a total quality management initiative, or the arrival of a new CEO. The next step involves deciding whether the compensation program should be changed and, if so, in what manner. For example, it may be preferable to introduce group incentives or offer stock to a broader base of employees in lieu of converting to broad band.

If broad band appears to be the correct mechanism for supporting business objectives, three activities should follow:

1. *Involve senior management.* It is not uncommon for the broad-banding process to begin with the top positions. But regardless of which jobs are included in the broad-band structure, senior management must completely support the idea if it is to be implemented successfully.

2. *Listen to employees.* This step may include focus groups, an employee survey, or a series of one-on-one interviews. Any latent employee-satisfaction issues or misdirected expectations should be uncovered and explored at the front end of the effort—not when the implementation process is under way.

3. *Assemble a design team.* This group is usually cross-functional, with enough experience and exposure to have a sound perspective on the objectives and culture of your business. The group will address a number of design, administrative, and communications issues at a series of meetings.

The design team produces a preliminary design that will need

Figure 11.2   Steps to Adopt Broad Banding

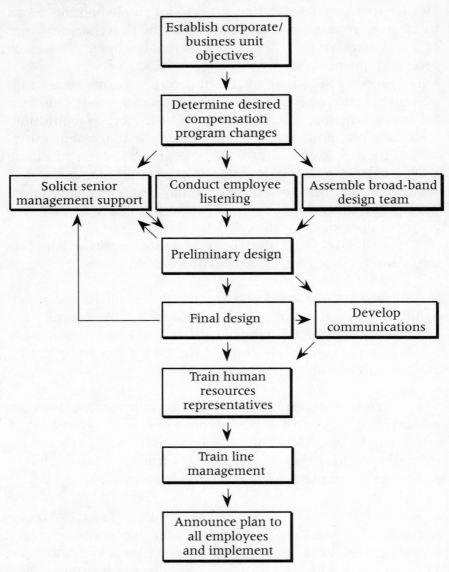

SOURCE: Hewitt Associates, LCC

to be reviewed by senior management. Additional employee listening sessions may also be desirable at this time to test reactions to the preliminary framework. The communications effort can also be initiated now, since many key features will be settled and will probably not change later on. Human resources professionals or consultants, such as Hewitt Associates, are typically involved in the design, communications, and training programs. From here, the training moves to line management and, ultimately, to the individual employees.

The overall time frame for this process may vary depending on the level of support for the program and the specific steps within the action plan. Most organizations require six months to two years to implement bands across a significant employee group.

Specific Implementation Issues

Any time a compensation program is changed, a number of administrative issues must be addressed. With a move to broad band, the administrative issues are even more pronounced, since the grading system (which is the traditional guide for eligibility for incentive plans, perquisites, and other benefits) will be replaced. Of course, most organizations that implement bands want to support a change in the culture of the organization. They are looking at the changes in the following areas as opportunities, not as unwanted side effects.

- *Job evaluation.* In most cases, the need for detailed quantitative job evaluation diminishes. It is far easier to determine what the correct band is when there are only five to choose from than it is to determine the correct salary grade when the evaluation process involves twenty-five grades.

- *Market pricing.* Market pricing is more important with broad band than with traditional salary structures. About half of Hewitt Associates' survey respondents expect their use of external market data to increase. This need is driven in part by the use of market data to determine pay targets within bands.

- *Midpoints.* Few companies retain the midpoint within a band, since it no longer represents the "market norm" for jobs within that band. In fact, 80 percent of survey respondents use no specific target or control point in the band to guide pay decisions. Instead, individual managers have wide flexibility to manage a person's pay within the band.

- *Salary budgeting.* Most companies manage pay by providing specific salary increase budgets to their managers. Promotions, six-month adjustments, and other pay-change budgets may be consolidated into a single figure. As long as managers do not exceed the budget, the program may be cost-neutral, and employees will not advance to unreasonable salary levels.

- *Job titles.* Many organizations that have delayered have also tried to simplify their job-titling system. This simplification is consistent with the goal of reducing status distinctions within the company. Since broad-band structures contain fewer levels, roughly half of all companies have changed their job titles concurrently with their transition to bands. Although some companies have been more successful than others in this area, this continues to be one of the most sensitive issues because employees place high emotional value on "earned" job titles and their associated prestige and internal power.

- *Incentive and perquisite eligibility.* In most cases, eligibility for incentive plans and perquisites is based on both conventional salary grade and additional independent criteria. These criteria are looked at when designing broad banding. Many companies determine that no changes in these eligibility criteria are needed. For this reason, when converting to broad banding, the impact on incentive or perquisite plans may be less than what might be expected.

Making the Decision to Change

The decision to implement broad banding should not be made casually. Although most companies do not introduce them solely to solve compensation issues, broad band significantly changes the way that managers and employees manage pay and pay expectations. Companies that have spent many years and considerable resources educating managers and employees about traditional pay programs should not abandon these programs without giving due consideration to other approaches, such as skill-based pay or results-sharing programs. Companies that are the strongest candidates for a successful broad-band system have the following characteristics:

- They want to support a new culture and most likely have just experienced a precipitous event.
- Top management strongly supports the change.
- Effective communications channels exist within the organization.
- Line managers are skilled at setting and managing employee pay.
- There is an effective performance management system in place.

Organizations that are least likely to benefit from converting to broad band may have some or all of the following characteristics:

- They may already be very successful with their current compensation programs.
- They may have a strong culture in place that values a traditional organizational hierarchy.

- They may have an effective career management system in place.

- Their current job structure already supports their business strategy.

- They may be looking to bands to solve salary administration issues such as the "topping out" of employees at the maximums of their salary ranges.

The use of broad bands will probably increase dramatically over the next several years. The success of these new programs will depend on the business and human resources goals they are intended to support and the care taken during the design effort.

Salary ranges without midpoints. Salary planning without a merit increase matrix. Supervisors and subordinates in the same pay level. It's the era of broad banding.

Broad banding (or salary banding) is one of the significant changes that is under way in salary administration along with skill-based pay, automation, and expanded use of variable pay. Many companies have implemented broad band in the past year or two and even more companies are exploring the feasibility of broad banding their traditional salary structures.

Is the Change to Broad Banding Worth It?

For most companies, broad banding represents an extraordinary cultural change. There are important considerations relating to job titles and promotion policies that may change when an organization introduces bands.

Those organizations that have introduced broad bands have done so because they believe broad bands make better business sense. Broad bands should bring the compensation program closer to an organization's decision making and manpower planning strategy in order to be most effective. Otherwise, it may be no better than the traditional salary structure it is replacing.

The use of broad bands will expand. In determining whether bands are appropriate for an organization, it is important to weigh the strategic effectiveness of the current system against the time and effort involved in implementing broad banding. Above all, an effective employee communications program is essential if the introduction of a broad-banding system is to be successful.

PAY-FOR-PERFORMANCE

As total quality management becomes the paradigm for customer satisfaction by business, the search for ways to integrate the performance management systems that became vogue in the 1970s and 1980s into the total quality management framework is being changed. Many business leaders have implemented at least one quality initiative, and most of these programs are less than five years old.

As business leaders, we need to find new ways to reward people for successfully implementing the new management tools, including total quality management, teamwork, world-class competitiveness, internal and external customer satisfaction, process improvement and flexibility. But a major change, such as scrapping compensation systems that have been used during the past two decades by installing some strange new pay system that leaves no room for individual evaluation or manager input, should be carefully examined before you start such a massive cultural change in your business.

Fortunately, there are different ways to implement reward systems that will complement your change management initiatives. Companies are examining combinations of individual merit-pay systems and teamwork systems; variable and fixed pay; fixed and nonrating systems; and gainsharing and individual incentive awards.

Steve Gross, the Hay Group's national director of variable

compensation, says what's most important in any pay program is
what one measures and rewards.[2] The best base-pay system will
measure behavioral competence, not accomplishments. The
pay-at-risk component of the reward system can be tied to accomplishment factors. In the model Gross likes to use, individuals are evaluated for base pay on such variables as ability to
communicate, customer focus, dealing with change, interpersonal skills, ability to work on a team, and professional and
technical knowledge. Managers are rated on employee development, group productivity, and leadership. Variable pay for both
managers and employees is based on what actually is accomplished. Variable pay can make up anywhere from 5 to 15 percent
of a total compensation package for those at the bottom of the
ladder, more at higher levels of the organization.

Because customer satisfaction is the core critical part of any
change effort, a three-category rating system can be implemented. The categories are: (1) not meeting customer expectations, (2) meeting them, or (3) far exceeding them. Those
employees who anticipate customer needs and actually develop
partnerships with their customers are the stars in the system.
Those who are just available and able to identify their customers
correctly get the average or "C" grade; and those who are non-
responsive and unwilling to support customers' needs get an "F."

It is important to remember that anyone your employees interact with is the "customer." So the model works for all parts of
the business, not just those divisions that actually deal with the
people who buy products or services.

Gross says that this type of system has several advantages.
The rules are known and communicated to all employees.
There is very little question about what types of behavior will
be rewarded. At the same time, the individual merit-based pay
that this country has traditionally used is not completely dis-
carded.

Many believe that merit pay is thought to foster an internal
competition within your business that is counterproductive to

your teamwork goals. Individual merit-based pay also may be grossly unfair, because it depends on the rating of a supervisor who may or may not like you. Some management gurus say individuals don't really control more than 20 percent of how they do their jobs, the rest depends on management systems and processes mandated in your system. If this is true, it's difficult to reward employees for individual efforts.

You can continue to use individual rewards, based on specific, well-thought-out criteria that reward competencies supporting your change initiative values. Reward the competencies you desire and use the variable pay component to spur employees on to greater productivity as teams.

In designing pay-for-performance programs, you must identify those factors that will lead to group success and then communicate and reward them. Such programs reinforce those values that benefit the company even if products or services change, employees have to work on different teams, or supervisors are promoted to new levels. Employees are not punished for factors that are not in their control—and the "turkeys," those 5 percent or so of employees whose work really is unsatisfactory, are dealt with through reassignment or termination.

In designing pay-for-performance systems, you must keep the ultimate goal of the rewards clearly in sight.[3] Towers Perrin consultants say companies should use rewards to obtain greater commitment, more flexibility, better cooperation and teamwork, more loyalty, better skills, improved productivity, and improved bottom line results. But employees who are also the customers of the reward program want greater security, more control, more fairness, greater choice, more input and more vision, clearer expectations, more frequent feedback, greater trust in management, the ability to make a difference, and more money.

To get employees to work better, management will have to communicate their shared vision, share information with employees at all levels to empower them, build trust and security through "walking the talk," and share the gains. Along the way, employers can reinforce the formation of teams as the basic elements of accomplishment.

Employers should evaluate and reward employees by using three perspectives:

- How they excel as individuals.
- How they function as part of primary performance unit.
- Where they fit in as citizens of the company.

Consultants have designed a variety of reward systems to meet these needs. Ultimately, pay-for-performance is only one part of a reward system designed to implement change management. Employers should think of a total reward strategy that includes such factors as comfort and security, understanding and recognition, influence and power, and, finally, pay and wealth.

Performance is no longer an individual phenomenon, but the product of how well we leverage skills into products or services. While in the past, quality may have been defined by focusing on individual contributions, now team incentives and performance rewards for teams take on much larger significance.

Measure the Right Stuff

To design a performance reward system that will positively impact your company, you must measure and reward the right elements. Steve Kerr, a performance rewards expert on the faculty of the University of Michigan's Graduate School of Business, has worked with General Electric Company to design effective ways to select, train, reward, and measure employees. Kerr says all measures should be tied to actions that directly affect one group of stakeholders—customers, employees, shareholders, or the public at large.

For example, measures of safety would be tied to actions that affect the public at large. Return on assets would affect shareholders. Quality measures would be tied to actions that affect customer satisfaction. And any number of measures that directly affect employees can be designed.

"Financial measures are where the rubber hits the road," Kerr says. But used by themselves, they are too easy to manipulate and leave employees feeling like spectators to the plan rather than a participant in the plan. Operational measures can be put in place sooner, evaluated sooner, and are subject to more control by employees. You need both to measure success effectively.

How to Design a Plan

In designing your pay-for-performance reward systems, the experts agree that certain basic elements must be present for success. These include:

- Communicating the plan well.

- Making sure that plan participants can indeed influence the measures by which the plan is evaluated.

- Having a consistent and fair plan.

- Making the rewards timely so participants feel the connection between the reward and the work.

- Having ample rewards to be distributed.

Business leaders often comment that building trust during this change process is one of the most important issues in determining a plan's success.

Those plans including task forces in their design, regardless of the level of employees serving on the task force, had ratings of higher satisfaction with improved teamwork than did those not using task forces. Management gave guidelines to the task force such as the plan objectives, type of award, eligible employee groups, payout measures, self-funding requirements, payout period, maximum payout, and plan introduction and deadlines.

Headquarters-mandated plans, which were primarily plans with financial measures, showed poor results in improving teamwork and cost the organization more in payouts.

It's impossible to give people enough information about such programs. There will always be people who don't get it. But communication is vitally important for a plan to succeed. People don't fear decisions they understand. These plans are about enablement and empowerment. They are broad-based, high-involvement, high-ownership programs. You have to engage your people in this change to make it work.

Questions about which systems work best and how they can be introduced into your business's specific culture are far from being definitively answered. There are only a finite number of rewards. What's needed is careful thought about how to distribute them to meet your specific business survival needs.

PAY-FOR-KNOWLEDGE

This book has described the pressing needs to increase your productivity. "Pay-for-knowledge"[4] is a concept that can help many business organizations improve their productivity with very little capital investment. Thomas J. Krajci, president of Resources for Management in Corning, New York, has described pay-for-knowledge as a sound management system to reward your employees, through direct payments, for their ability to perform an operationally related array of tasks or skills rather than for the actual work performed at any given time.

The pay-for-knowledge approach can improve significantly your flexibility and capacity to respond to changing demands and schedules. Employees who have mastered additional work or job skills receive added pay for this knowledge even if they are not currently performing those tasks. Rewarding an individual for additional capabilities creates a more flexible workforce than does pay-for-performance, which rewards (merit pay, bonus) only what is actually accomplished rather than what can be done.

A pay-for-knowledge system can benefit an organization in significant ways:

- ❏ Fewer job classifications.

- ❏ Greater workforce flexibility and productivity.

- ❏ Higher employee motivation to acquire additional work skills.

- ❏ Reduced "turf battles" within a job family.

- ❏ Improved employee morale.

Implementation

To implement pay-for-knowledge, a specific set of procedures is necessary, as described below.

1. *Analyze and describe jobs.* A sound job evaluation system is crucial to installing a pay-for-knowledge program. Accurate, up-to-date job descriptions that focus on the major tasks of each position are the first step in developing a database of job duties that will later be combined into job families.

Descriptions should be brief and to the point. Employees and supervisors then review them to ensure total agreement on their accuracy. Great weight should be given to the employees' descriptions of their actual duties.

2. *Evaluate jobs.* A team of managers who are knowledgeable about the operation and represent a cross-section of its departments and divisions then evaluates all jobs individually, using a

point-factor job evaluation process. The team members should have the professional respect of all levels of employees to ensure confidence in the results.

The evaluation team must work toward complete agreement on each position it evaluates. Each team member needs the opportunity to state reasons for disagreement with other members on a particular factor.

3. *Develop wage structure.* Once the evaluation process is completed for all jobs, develop and implement a competitive—that is, market driven—pay structure. Even though jobs will later be combined and the number of classifications reduced, the organization first needs a sound pay structure for all jobs.

The pay structure is based on a combination of quantitative statistical analysis and the particular qualitative factors the organization uses to assess internal relationships and equity.

4. *Identify job families.* While the competitive pay structure is being developed, analyze individual jobs and organize them into a logical, operational grouping of jobs and job families. The jobs to be combined must make sense to the operating personnel and their supervisors.

For example, in developing a pay structure for a manufacturer of proprietary instruments, a logical grouping of jobs and tasks may comprise five assembly positions that had previously been considered separate and distinct.

5. *Group tasks.* Using the approved job descriptions, identify elements common to all members of a job family and those unique to each specific job. From this, create a master job description for each job family or grouping. In the assembler example, five different assembly jobs were combined into a master description with eighteen major elements.

6. *Develop relative weights.* As a result of the job evaluation process in step 2, each job has evaluation points that the commit-

tee determines which are used to develop individual pay rates in the pay structure. In this phase, the evaluation committee assigns relative weights (using 500 to 1,000 points) without regard to the job evaluation process in step 2.

The evaluation committee then develops a rank ordering and relative weighing for each of the duties of the master family or group job description. Each job description should be allocated the same number of points (five hundred or one thousand) to spread across all of the duties in its master family description.

Do not confuse the two point values. The point value derived from the job evaluation manual is for setting equitable pay rates and pay structures.

This relative weighing technique is unique to each master description and is used to establish the pay-for-knowledge pay rate for a specific job family or job grouping, as opposed to the overall pay structure.

7. *Determine job knowledge.* Once the committee is satisfied that the relative internal ratings of points and values are valid, the next step is to have each supervisor evaluate the capability of each employee to perform each task in the master job description.

For an employee to receive the assigned point value, he or she must be capable of performing the task at the minimum acceptable quality and speed. The employee should not receive partial credit: the employee either can perform the task correctly and acceptably or needs additional training that your business would provide.

A data-collection form unique to each master description will enable supervisors to quickly complete the knowledge evaluation process.

8. *Establish matrices.* Establish a matrix of job duties, relative weighing points, incumbent personnel and their current pay. Enter the point value for each job duty, to arrive at each employee's total knowledge points. These points represent the employee's total knowledge and ability to perform these duties.

And hence their value to the organization in direct proportion to the assigned point value (relative weight).

9. *Create pay ranges.* Identify the minimum core of skills that all members of the job family possess or should possess. This establishes the minimum point value of the pay range and will also be valuable in establishing a training method for each job family so that a new employee can quickly reach acceptable performance levels.

The maximum knowledge point value is normally defined by the total possible knowledge point value, either 500 or 1,000 points. The average performance or normal skill level for the job family will usually fall at about the midpoint value level (250 or 500 points). Convert this point level to dollars from the competitive pay structure developed previously.

From these dollar levels, develop the minimum and maximum pay for the knowledge-range limits for each job family or grouping. It may be necessary to adjust the range and values to arrive at an acceptable minimum and maximum.

It may be advantageous to establish a training period for new employees, with a training rate that is adjusted as soon as the employee can perform the minimum acceptable core of job duties for the job family.

10. *Determine practicality.* Test the practicality of the system by converting each incumbent's knowledge point values (previously determined by the supervisors in step 7 above) into wages and salaries. Compare these trial rates of pay with each incumbent's actual pay. Software spreadsheet analysis is ideal for this type of analysis and decision making.

11. *Develop implementation plan.* This system will highlight deficiencies in the past administration of wages and salaries. Past errors will have created an imbalance of highly compensated individuals with relatively low knowledge evaluation points or vice versa.

Resolving Disputes

Employees must be able to appeal a supervisor's evaluation and obtain an objective determination of individual job knowledge. On-the-job performance will resolve nearly all of these problems, and any pay adjustments can be made retroactive to the date of the original evaluation.

The presence of a union will make the appeal process more complicated because of the grievance arbitration process. However, patience and a rapid on-the-job performance test will normally resolve the dispute.

While individuals receiving an upward pay adjustment will be pleased, resolving the problems of those who are "red-circled" and receiving pay beyond their demonstrated job knowledge skill level will test the pay-for-knowledge system and your organization. Red-circled employees should be given a period of time in which to increase their job family knowledge, and hence their value to the organization before their pay is reduced. Pay freezes, attrition, or phased-in reductions may help bring overpaid individuals in line with the new pay structure.

In general, employees like the system, if they have a way to question their supervisor's evaluations and if pay is actually adjusted—up or down—to match demonstrated job knowledge.

Making It Work

Each business needs to carefully consider the advantages of a pay-for-knowledge system. If the organization has related jobs and must shift people around to fill a changing work schedule, then it may consider implementing a pay-for-knowledge system.

A pay-for-knowledge system must include a procedure for objectively adjudicating employee complaint about supervisory evaluations. Failure to adopt a procedure for hearing and resolving employee challenges can lead to serious, if not fatal, problems with the system. Equally important is obtaining supervisory support for a pay-for-knowledge system. If both are absent the system will surely fail.

No reward system is perfect. Therefore, it is essential that pay-for-performance be adapted to the unique needs of the organization and tested to ensure that it will remain practical and workable. Continuous testing following implementation will help maintain a fair and equitable system that can have significant benefits for your business.

CHAPTER 12

An Action Guide for Survival

One of the problems leaders face today is the need for them to develop a clear, simple, road map or plan of action, when there are so many different management techniques to select from to improve their performance.

IMMEDIATE PERFORMANCE IMPROVEMENT ACTIONS

This chapter provides an action plan in the form of a ten-step immediate performance improvement methodology that is based on the ten key survival factors described in chapter 3. The priority for near-term action is delineated in table 12.1.

In order for you to begin to adopt the immediate performance improvement steps described in this chapter, you should first assess your current needs for improvement. As part of chapter 2, a self-assessment is provided under the subheading "Do You Need a Survival Plan?" The ten action steps described in this chapter are provided as a set of steps for your near-term action. However, if your self-assessment indicates that you are already

Table 12.1 Immediate Performance Improvement Priority Action

PRIORITY	ACTION ELEMENT
1	Demonstrate your leadership
2	Stop the bleeding
3	Cut your costs
4	Satisfy your customers
5	Do it right the first time
6	Reengineer your processes
7	Walk the talk
8	Apply technology
9	Continue to improve
10	Keep it simple

addressing some of these steps, proceed to the appropriate action step. Beware of the urge to say, "We have already done that" for one of the steps, when, in fact, your assessment of your operation shows that more effort in certain areas is really required.

Each of the immediate performance improvement steps is described below.

Demonstrate Your Leadership

Leadership requires the development of shared values, the ability to communicate your vision, and for you to actively "practice what you preach." The lack of top management leadership and active participation is the main reason that quality management, reengineering, product and process improvement, and business improvement efforts created to help your business survive fail.

As noted in *The West Point Ways of Leadership*, leadership is "the philosophy and *practice* of a set of values. Standing in mud with your people, learning their work, staying with their problems until solutions are found."[1]

Figure 12.1 identifies the three key action elements you need to focus on to demonstrate your leadership.

Figure 12.1   Demonstrate Your Leadership Actions

273

When Jack Welch of General Electric took charge, he needed to address the significant changes necessary for General Electric's survival in a new global market. He examined those action items under his near-term and immediate control and developed a plan of attack or vision of what needed to be done at General Electric. He started by examining the financial and product market elements. His early vision concentrated on being a value-driven market leader, which required downsizing General Electric and eliminating products or services that were not in the top two or three positions in their market.

You will need to examine your business and develop your own vision and strategic approach for change. Once you know where you must lead your business, you can continually communicate where you and the business are in terms of meeting your performance improvement goals. This is not a one-time executive decree. You must constantly reinforce your vision and lead by example to encourage risk taking and change by your employees. As new people are included in your improvement efforts, you will need to reeducate them as to your goals and needs. It is a never-ending battle to assure that a clear, simple message is communicated to every employee.

It is not enough for you to sign the executive order or policy manual change and walk away from your real responsibilities to change the way your company has been doing business. You must actively participate, oversee, and check to assure that your guidance is being implemented. Some leaders fail because they underestimate the time it takes for your employees to "get the message." You have to get out of the corporate tower and join the battle for survival in every element of your business.

Stop the Bleeding

The first rule of first aid is to stop the bleeding. For your business, the major artery that must be healed is your financial situation in terms of poor products or services and cost mismanagement practices that may be causing your business to hemorrhage.

Figure 12.2 identifies four key elements for your immediate action to stop the bleeding.

When you take charge of an existing business, you need to assess your financial performance, your market performance in terms of market share, your operational performance in terms of process effectiveness and productivity, and your customer and supplier relationships.

These assessments for a large company can take six to nine months; for a small business, you might need one to two months. The caution is for you to act decisively now, instead of examining your problems forever. You need to demonstrate a new leadership position quickly. You can attack at once by developing a clear plan to review your current state-of-the-practice, benchmark your competitive performance, get rid of marginal business elements, and rebundle your business operations.

One of the best and easiest starting points is to visit and meet every major business unit manager, to determine for yourself the extent of the problems your business must address to assure your survival. Create teams to review issues of financial concern, product marketability, cost and productivity performance. By knowing your real current situation, you can create your plan of attack with fewer false starts and inaccurate assumptions.

As described in chapter 4, benchmark your product or services against your competitors. Without obtaining a reasonable view of the gap in performance between yourself and your competitors, you will not be able to develop an effective strategy for survival.

As part of your strategic vision, you should plan on downsizing or eliminating poor-performing business units as soon as possible.

Figure 12.2   Stop the Bleeding Actions

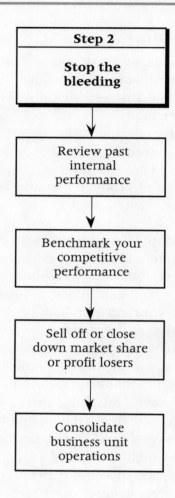

This means selling off or closing down market share or profit losers. Reduce the number of marginal products so you can assure adequate attention to your survival-focused products and services. Elimination of major business units and product lines is one of the areas as leader you may have the greatest near-term impact on. And, in many cases, it is one of the "executive" actions that you can really directly control.

Once you have begun to develop your "lean" business, start to create teams to examine your processes as described in chapter 5. By gaining a better understanding of your process problems, you can effectively begin to consolidate the remaining business units to support your vision, and inspire change.

Cut Your Costs

As your business is driven to compete more aggressively on the basis of quality, time to market, flexible production, and product and service innovation, you will have to provide better value to your customers. That means you will have to aggressively cut your costs, as shown in figure 12.3.

Traditional economic cost assessment and reduction techniques are a good near-term starting point. However, to take advantage of the real gains in providing value to your customers, you will also need to focus on the noneconomic "noncost" or intangible benefits. Some of these noneconomic issues include retention of your customer base, reduced lead time impacts on overall costs, reduction of the number of process steps, ability to satisfactorily meet delivery schedules, ability to provide product or services to your customers that "work," overhead and administrative cost reduction, as well as traditional direct labor cost reductions, facility cost savings due to reduction in floor space and environmental control costs.

Begin by examining your business processes as described in chapter 5, and if more aggressive cost cutting is required, begin to reengineer "bottleneck" processes as described in chapter 8.

Figure 12.3   Cut Your Cost Actions

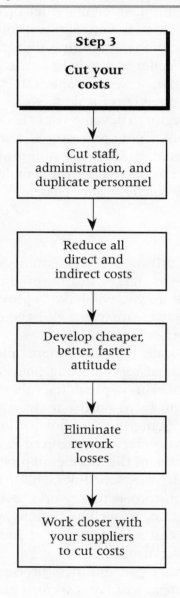

Step 3

Cut your costs

Cut staff,
administration, and
duplicate personnel

Reduce all
direct and
indirect costs

Develop cheaper,
better, faster
attitude

Eliminate
rework
losses

Work closer with
your suppliers
to cut costs

Cuts in most direct labor operations have already taken place in many businesses. The key today is to aggressively cut corporate staff, administration, sales, and duplicate human resources, public affairs, and other nonessential personnel.

A new attitude needs to be instilled in your employees to stress development of less costly products and services, faster development and delivery of products and services, and to provide reliable products to your customers. This paradigm shift toward cheaper, better, and faster will help facilitate change in your business. For manufacturing business, the cost of doing it over can be 20 to 40 percent of your product delivery costs. For information systems, the rework may be up to 60 percent of your costs. By adopting total quality management as described in chapter 6, you can reduce your rework by doing the job right the first time.

All too often, we think of cost cutting in terms of our internal operations. Significant cost cutting, with less emotional turmoil for your own business, can be obtained by reexamining your relationships with your suppliers. By working with your suppliers, you can obtain near-term reductions in your costs, and build a relationship that encourages continuous productivity improvements and cost reductions while improving the reliability and quality of the products or services that you buy.

Satisfy Your Customers

Business survival begins and ends by your satisfying your customers. No customers, no business. Therefore, it is surprising how few businesses know who their customers really are, and if their customers are satisfied with the products and services you provide.

As shown in figure 12.4, there are five key actions you should implement now to satisfy your customers.

As noted above, many business leaders think they know who their customers are and what they expect in terms of value. But in business after business, we find that only a partial picture of

Figure 12.4   Satisfy Your Customer Actions

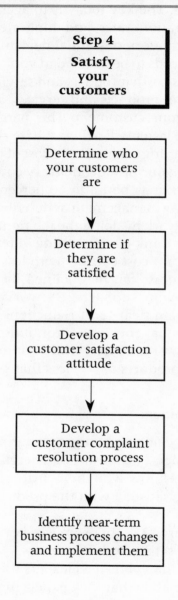

who your customers are is known. But it is even more important for the growth of your business for you to understand why clients may have left you, or why potential new clients ignore your products or services.

You need to get closer to your customers by conducting selected personal visits by yourself and your key employees to see the real-world use of your products and services. Also, there is a need for better measurement of your ongoing performance by focus groups and other performance surveys to assess the broader market, and the impact of your changes in operation over time.

Two actions that are easily implemented in the near-term to improve customer satisfaction are (1) the improvement in the communication skills and attitude of your employees in their interaction with your customers and (2) the development of an effective complaint-handling system to retain current customers. The revitalization of your operation is partially based on your customers' perception of how you do business. Changing your employees' attitudes toward your customers is not necessarily easy, but it must be done for you to survive in this "customer focus"–oriented market.

In the near-term, as a result of your customer assessment, act quickly to implement basic changes that your customers have identified. You need to demonstrate change, and prompt action demonstrates the new approach that you are aggressively implementing to keep your current customer base. Refer to chapter 5 to examine and improve your processes, and chapter 6 to implement total quality management.

Do It Right the First Time

In terms of priority action, you may need to develop and implement total quality management in your business. Depending on your business, you may already have a mature quality management approach instilled in your operations. If so, you need to continue your quality improvement activities as part of step 9.

However, many businesses have given only lip service to satisfying their customers and improving their business by adopting
quality management concepts. Figure 12.5 shows the action steps
you should examine to improve your quality and reduce rework.

To reduce rework, improve productivity, and enhance your
customer service begin by examining and understanding your
processes. As noted in chapter 5, map your processes, starting
from the end of the process outcome and working backward to
identify critical "bottlenecks" that can be evaluated and improved quickly. Most leaders, responsible for a task activity,
know where the ongoing "bottlenecks" are that cause production delays, process delays, and customer problems. Their task is
to communicate the problem to a larger multifunctional group
that can help resolve the problem.

Chapter 4 provides a methodology for you to benchmark your
processes within your business, in your industry, and with your
competitors. Benchmarking can help you see new near-term
opportunities to improve your business processes.

Once you know what needs to be improved, adopt the total
quality management concepts described in chapter 6. It is important to develop a balanced total quality management approach
tailored to your own unique needs. There isn't a standard cookie-
cutter approach that you can copy directly. Based on your customer needs, organizational difficulties, and employee situation,
you will need to create a total quality management effort that
focuses both on tools and techniques *and* cultural attitude change.

Rework can be killing your business. Once you have examined
your process, look for every feasible way to simplify your product
design, service delivery, and administrative work flow processes.

Reengineer Your Processes

If your business is on the verge of financial collapse, you may not
have time to reengineer your operations, as shown in figure 12.6.

However, if you do have eighteen months to turn around

Figure 12.5   Do It Right the First Time Actions

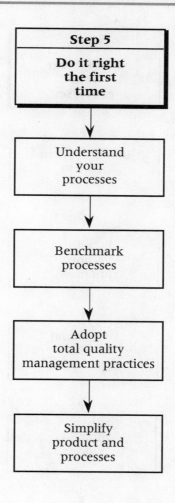

Figure 12.6   Reengineer Your Process Actions

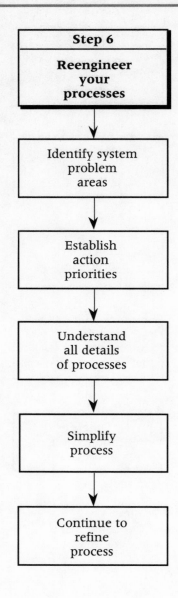

your business, or if your business is strong and you want to move to the next level of competitive management skills, you could examine enterprise-wide business process reengineering (BPR), product reengineering, or substantial process reengineering as shown in figure 12.6 and as described more fully in chapter 8.

If you are going to reengineer, start by identifying your critical management, financial, or process bottlenecks and business systemic problems.

Using analytical tools, such as Pareto diagrams, rank order the most effective (impact on cost reduction, productivity, and business survival issue) action priorities. Reengineering is a wrenching change in the way you have done business. After identifying priorities and policy and strategic concerns carefully, understand all the details of the significant process changes you are about to make. Don't rush into new technology, new automation, new information systems, or new improved processes because some consultant or peer thought it would be an interesting exercise. Change because it is in your business's best interest.

Once you are ready to implement your reengineering activity, reexamine and make sure you understand the details of the impending changes, then proceed to simplify and reengineer these priority processes.

Some businesses think that the reengineering effort is a one-time improvement in your business. But like total quality management, you will need to continue to reengineer as your competitors, business environment, and processes continue to change.

Walk the Talk

Constancy of purpose is the phrase used by the quality gurus to emphasize constant leadership participation in your change process. Figure 12.7 identifies four steps to help reinforce your role as the leader of change in your business.

Earlier in this chapter, we discussed the need for you to lead by example. This leadership requires your deep personal commit-

Figure 12.7   Walk the Talk Actions

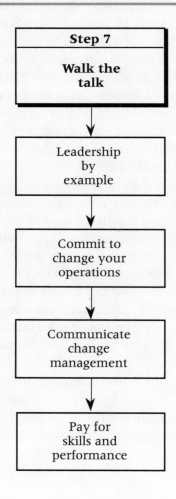

ment to change your operations. It isn't easy, it isn't painless, it isn't fun; but it is necessary for your business to survive.

You can't delegate your visible support and consistent action to your subordinates; you have to do it yourself. You must in every meeting, in every talk, in every memo be consistent in communicating the need to change, and your support for your employees who are changing.

In addition to talking a good story, you must support reward and recognition efforts that show your interest in change by your employees who have joined your challenge to survive. In concert with the management team, you need to explore ways to motivate your team members. You may be able to implement realistic, logical, fair, pay-for-performance, and pay-for-learning initiatives for your employees. Chapter 10 addresses building your teams, and chapter 11 describes the opportunity for you to develop and implement new pay systems for your business.

Apply Appropriate Technology

New robots, computer information systems, or related tools by themselves will not improve your chance for survival, if they are poorly conceived, inadequately justified, or poorly implemented.

Hunt's first rule of technology is "Don't implement new technology if your task can be done without it." All too often we jump to the technology fix that can complicate our fight for survival. Therefore, as noted in figure 12.8, first determine if process changes can be done as well without new technology. Maybe the process step can be eliminated altogether by reengineering your operations.

If you really need to add new technology, don't be the flag carrier for new, unproven technology. Make sure the technology works in similar operations and only apply the minimum level of technology needed to address your problem.

During the past decade, technology has focused on "islands of improvement" rather than overall improvement of your business enterprise. Look for integrated systems that exchange data

Figure 12.8   Technology Application Actions

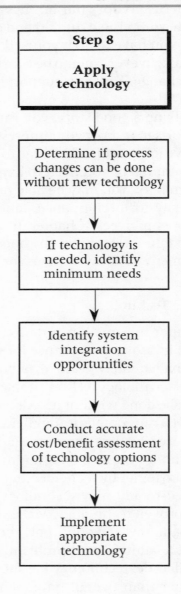

among a diverse set of technology platforms. Open system configurations will help ensure that your technology investment will outlast the relatively short life of most technology innovations. By focusing on system integration opportunities as noted in chapter 9, you will gain the synergetic benefits of technology application that meets your basic needs.

Avoid being "sold" a technology fix that is not cost-effective for your needs. Review both the economic and noneconomic benefits of various technology options. Concentrate on assessing technology (hardware and software) that you can apply today. Avoid complex, multipurpose technology that is beyond your immediate technology needs.

Once you have assessed the full benefits of the new technology, develop a plan for implementation that includes all aspects of successful application, including sufficient operator training and maintenance support.

For some business leaders, the problem is not applying excessively complex technology, but the failure to apply or lack of the minimum level of technology to assure productive operations. In some businesses, investment in simple personal computers can improve customer service or production processes. This problem is more often found in service businesses rather than manufacturing. You need to make the capital investments to support your service business processes even more than in manufacturing.

The key is to implement the appropriate level of proven technology that will enhance your productivity and specific process improvement efforts.

Continue to Improve

The Japanese term for improvement is *kaizen*. It means continuing improvement involving everyone—executives, mid-level managers, blue-collar and white-collar workers alike. Continuous improvement concentrates on gradual, unending improvement, doing "little things" better, and setting and achieving ever-higher goals and standards of performance.

Figure 12.9 reflects the Plan-Do-Check-Act (PDCA) cycle. The PDCA cycle asserts that every managerial action can be improved by careful application of this sequence of action.

The "Plan" step addresses the need to build consensus and think through the anticipated changes. The action step is to "Just do it." Then the "Check" phase measures your performance and provides feedback to repeat your improvement process. Continuous process improvement can help you and your team obtain your stretch goals and improve your day-to-day near-term and long-term performance.

Keep It Simple

The last step in our methodology to improve your performance is based on the KISS principle. That is, "Keep it simple, stupid."

Complex survival plans are very difficult to communicate and implement in your business. As in the case of General Electric, for their second phase of realignment their change initiative focused on only three elements, which they identified as (1) workout—to encourage communication and change, (2) best practices—to benchmark their performance, and (3) process mapping—to understand and simplify their processes. As shown in figure 12.10, the key for business leaders is to focus on what is critical for your survival. There are hundreds of things to do during the revitalization of your business. But you can become distracted and waste valuable time and resources if you divert your attention away from the critical elements of survival. Therefore, do only what is required to assure your survival.

During the last decade, we have seen voluminous strategic plans, handsomely bound, and collecting dust in executive bookcases. Create a small, realistic, integrated plan for your business. Produce a living plan that is part of your daily operational management process.

Figure 12.9   Action to Continue Improvement

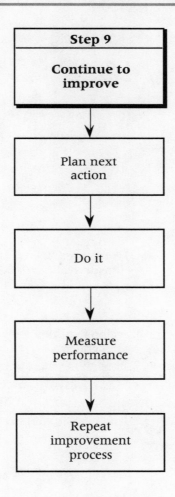

Figure 12.10   Keep It Simple

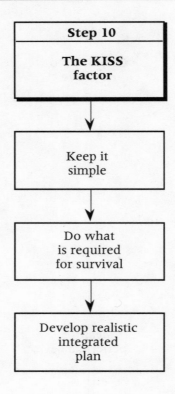

IMMEDIATE PERFORMANCE
IMPROVEMENT MATRIX

Figure 12.11 provides a matrix of the immediate performance improvement steps as they relate to the management tools described in chapters 2 through 11.

Depending on your current business situation, select the priority areas for immediate action and refer to the chapter crosswalk shown in figure 12.11 to develop your own customized approach for survival.

Figure 12.11   Immediate Performance Matrix

ACTION STEP	ACTION ELEMENT	REFERRAL CHAPTER									
		2	3	4	5	6	7	8	9	10	11
1	Demonstrate your leadership	X	X						X	X	X
2	Stop the bleeding				X		X				
3	Cut your costs					X	X	X			
4	Satisfy your customer			X		X					
5	Do it right the first time			X	X	X			X		
6	Reengineer your processes					X		X	X	X	
7	Walk the talk					X	X		X		
8	Apply technology							X	X		
9	Continue to improve					X	X				X
10	Keep it simple		X			X	X				

CHAPTER 13

Tomorrow, Tomorrow, Tomorrow

There is no tomorrow! To survive the rapidly changing market, you must begin to change today.

Notes

Chapter 1   To Survive—Act Now!

1. *The Handbook for Decline* is an abridged version of material (pp. 270–72) from *Profits in the Dark—How Xerox Reinvented Itself and Beat Back the Japanese*, by David T. Kearns and David A. Nadler. HarperBusiness, New York, 1992. Reprinted by permission of HarperBusiness.
2. *Ibid.*
3. *Ibid.*

Chapter 2   Develop Your Own Survival Plan

1. Bruce Henderson, *Harvard Business Review*. "The Origins of Strategy; Nov.–Dec. 1989, Boston, Mass.
2. *Post-Capitalist Society*, Peter F. Drucker. New York: Harper-Business, 1993.
3. *Ibid.*
4. *The West Point Way of Leadership*, Larry R. Donnithorne. New York: Currency Doubleday, 1993.
5. Self assessment based on the Malcolm Baldrige National Quality Questionnaire from *The Journal for Quality and Participation*, June 1990.

Chapter 3   The Ten Key Survival Factors

1. *The West Point Way of Leadership*, Larry R. Donnithorne. New York: Currency Doubleday, 1993.
2. *Total Quality Control for Management: Strategies and Tactics from Toyota and Toyota Gosei*, David Lu, ed. and trans. Englewood Cliffs, NJ: Prentice Hall, 1987.
3. *Control Your Destiny or Someone Else Will*, Noel M. Tichy and Stratford Sherman. New York: Currency Doubleday, 1993.
4. *Current Practices in Measuring Quality*, Research Bulletin No. 234. New York: The Conference Board, Inc., 1989.
5. *The PIMS Letter on Business Strategy*. Report No. 4. Cambridge, MA: The Strategic Planning Institute, 1986.
6. *Quality*, Noriaki Kano. Union of Japanese Scientists and Engineers, Tokyo, April 1, 1983.
7. *Reengineering the Corporation*, Michael Hammer and James Champy. New York: Harper Collins Publishers, 1993.
8. *Reengineering—Leveraging the Power of Integrated Product Development*, V. Daniel Hunt. Essex Junction, VT: Oliver Wight/ Omneo, 1993.
9. "Who Needs a Boss?," Brian Dumaine, *Fortune*, May 7, 1990.
10. *Ibid*.

Chapter 4   Benchmark Your Performance

1. *Competitive Benchmarking: What It Is and What It Can Do For You*. Stamford, CT: Xerox Corporate Quality Office, 1987.
2. *Competitive Benchmarking: The Path to a Leadership Position*. Stamford, CT: Xerox Corporate Quality Office, 1988.
3. *Leadership Through Quality Training Programs: A Guide to Benchmarking in Xerox*. Available through a partnership with the U.S. Department of Commerce, National Technical Information Services (NTIS), Springfield, VA 22152. The NTIS document number is PB91-780106.
4. *Ibid*.

5. *Ibid.*
6. *Ibid.*
7. *Competitive Benchmarking.*
8. *Ibid.*
9. *Ibid.*
10. *Quality in America—How to Implement a Competitive Quality Program*, V. Daniel Hunt. Burr Ridge, IL: Irwin Professional Publishing, 1992.

Chapter 5   Understand Your Business Processes

1. The continuous process improvement steps in this chapter are based on *An Introduction to the Continuous Improvement Process—Principles and Practices*, by Nicholas R. Schacht and Brian E. Mansir, April 1989, developed by LMI under DoD contract MDA903-85-C-0139. We thank DoD and LMI for permission to use this material, which has been revised to emphasize the role of continuous process improvement in business survival situations.
2. *Dynamic Manufacturing—Creating the Learning Organization*, Robert H. Hayes, Steven C. Wheelwright, and Kim B. Clark. New York: The Free Press, 1988.
3. *Reengineering—Leveraging the Power of Integrated Product Development*, V. Daniel Hunt. Essex Junction, VT: Oliver Wight/Omneo, 1993.
4. *Control Your Destiny or Someone Else Will*, Noel M. Tichy and Stratford Sherman. New York: Currency Doubleday, 1993.

Chapter 6   Don't Do It Again and Again

1. *Quality in America—How to Implement a Competitive Quality Program*, V. Daniel Hunt. Burr Ridge, IL: Irwin Professional Publishing, 1992.
2. *A Guide for Implementing Total Quality Management*, Reliability

Analysis Center state-of-the-art report. Report SOAR-7, Rome, NY, Rome AFB, 1990.

3. *Leadership Through Quality Training Programs: A Guide to Benchmarking in Xerox.* U.S. Department of Commerce, National Technical Information Service (NTIS), Springfield, VA. NTIS Report Number PB91-780106.

Chapter 7   The Downsizing Trend

1. Portions of the cover story entitled *"The Pain of Downsizing,"* from the May 9, 1994 issue of *Business Week*, has been reproduced with the permission of McGraw-Hill. The commentary from this article was by John A. Byrne.
2. *Ibid.*

Chapter 8   Reengineer Your Business

1. *Reengineering the Corporation*, Michael Hammer and James Champy. New York: Harper Collins Publishers, 1993.
2. *Reengineering—Leveraging the Power of Integrated Product Development*, V. Daniel Hunt. Essex Junction, VT: Oliver Wight/ Omneo, 1993.

Chapter 10   Empower Your Team

1. *Reengineering—Leveraging the Power of Integrated Product Development*, V. Daniel Hunt, Essex Junction, VT: Oliver Wight/ Omneo, 1993.
2. The author acknowledges the excellent work of Dan Stone of the USDA in his efforts to delineate the key self assessment criteria that can improve performance. This self assessment is an abridgement/modification of his work.

Chapter 11   Pay for Skills and Performance

1. The author thanks Kenan S. Abosch for providing information on broad banding. The material in this chapter is an

abridgement of Hewitt Associates LLC material on broad banding. Hewitt Associates LLC is the leading authority on broad banding. For more information, contact Mr. Abosch at Hewitt Associates, 100 Half Day Road, Lincolnshire, IL 60069, (708) 295-5000.

2. *Pay for Performance—What You Should Know*, by Linda Thornburg, June 1992, reprinted with the permission of *HRMagazine*, published by the Society for Human Resource Management, Alexandria, VA.

3. *How Do You Cut the Cake?*, by Linda Thornburg, October 1992, reprinted with the permission of *HRMagazine*, published by the Society for Human Resource Management, Alexandria, VA.

4. *Pay That Rewards Knowledge*, by Thomas J. Krajci, June 1990, reprinted with the permission of *HRMagazine*, published by the Society for Human Resource Management, Alexandria, VA.

Chapter 12   An Action Guide for Survival

1. *The West Point Way of Leadership*, Larry R. Donnithorne. New York: Currency Doubleday, 1993.

Suggested Readings

AT&T Quality Steering Committee, "Reengineering Handbook." Baskin Ridge, New Jersey: AT&T, 1993.

Balm, Gerald J. *Benchmarking: A Practitioner's Guide for Becoming and Staying Best of the Best*. Schaumberg, IL: Quality and Productivity Management Association, 1992.

Bennis, Warren, and Burt Nanus. *Leaders: The Strategies for Taking Charge*. New York: Harper & Row, 1985.

Camp, Robert C. *Benchmarking: The Search for Industry Best Practices That Lead to Superior Performance*. Milwaukee: WI: Quality Press/American Society for Quality Control, 1989.

Davenport, Thomas H. "Process Innovation—Reengineering Work through Information Technology." Boston: Harvard Business School Press, 1993.

Drucker, Peter F. *Managing for the Future—The 1990's and Beyond*. New York: Truman Talley Books/Dutton, 1992.

Drucker, Peter F. *Post-Capitalist Society*. New York: HarperBusiness, 1993.

Ernst and Young. *Guide to Total Cost Management*. New York: John Wiley and Sons, 1992.

Hammer, Michael, and James Champy. *Reengineering the Corporation—A Manifesto for Business Revolution*. New York: Harper Collins Publishers, 1993.

Hayes, Robert H., Steven C. Wheelwright, and Kim B. Clark. *Dynamic Manufacturing*. New York: The Free Press, 1988.

Hunt, V. Daniel. *Computer Integrated Manufacturing Handbook*. New York: Chapman and Hall, 1989.

————. *Quality in America*. Burr Ridge, IL: Irwin Professional Publishing (Business One Irwin), 1992.

————. *Reengineering—Leveraging the Power of Integrated Product Development*, Essex Junction, VT: Oliver Wight/Omneo, 1993.

Imai, Masaki. *Kaizen: The Key to Japan's Competitive Success*. New York: Random House, 1986.

Ishikawa, Kaoru. *What Is Total Quality Control? The Japanese Way*. Englewood Cliffs, NJ: Prentice Hall, 1985.

Juran, Joseph M. *Juran on Planning for Quality*. New York: McGraw-Hill, 1988.

Malcolm Baldrige National Quality Award, 1994 Award Criteria, U.S. Department of Commerce, National Institute of Standards and Technology, Gaithersburg, MD.

Noer, David M. *Healing the Wounds: Overcoming the Trauma of Layoffs and Revitalized Downsized Organizations*. San Francisco: CA, Jossey Bass, 1993.

Peterson, Donald E. *A Better Idea—Redefining the Way Americans Work*. Boston, MA: Houghton Mifflin, 1991.

Rodgers, T. J., William Taylor, and Rick Foreman. *No-Excuses Management*. New York: Currency Doubleday, 1992.

Scholtes, Peter R., et al. *The Team Handbook—How to Use Teams to Improve Quality*. Madison, WI: Joiner Associates, 1988.

Stalk, George, and Thomas M. Hout. *Competing Against Time*. New York: The Free Press, 1990.

Tomasko, Robert M. *Downsizing—Reshaping the Corporation for the Future*. New York: AMACOM, 1990.

Watson, Gregory H. *Strategic Benchmarking*. New York: John Wiley & Sons, 1993.

Wheelright, Steven C., and Kim B. Clark. *Revolutionizing Product Development*. New York: The Free Press, 1992.

Index

Process improvement (*cont.*)
  see also Continuous process
    improvement; Quality
    processes; Reengineering
Process mapping (PMAP), for
    process improvement, 110–15,
    120
Procter & Gamble, teams at, 65
Product design, failure from
    ignoring, 5
Product development, reengineering
    and, 62–63
Productivity improvement, 210–14
  as critical success factor, 14
  importance of, 15
  pay systems based on, 19, *see also*
    Pay-for-knowledge
  system integrated automation
    technology and, 211, 213–21
  technology for, 211–13
Profits in the Dark (Kearns), 4
Promotions, broad banding
    deemphasizing, 248

Quality
  benchmarking lowering cost of,
    76
  cost of, 133–35
  failure from ignoring, 4
  reengineering focusing on, 197
  self-assessment of, 36–39
  senior management taking action
    on, 49
  see also Benchmarking; Customer-
    driven quality; Customer
    satisfaction; Process
    improvement; Total quality
    management
Quality champion, for total quality
    management, 137–38
Quality Council, for total quality
    management, 143–45
Quality improvement teams, 129

Quality management
  as immediate performance action,
    281–82, 283
  as survival factor, 58–61
Quality metrics, in benchmarking,
    84
Quality processes, building as core
    survival attribute, 27

Recalibration, in benchmarking, 91
Recognition
  broad banding and, 248
  in total quality management, 130–
    31, 143, 159–61
Reengineering, 7, 20, 25, 188–208
  advantages of, 192–93
  automated systems and, 216–17
  business process, 190, 191, 197,
    284, 285
  continuous process improvement
    for, 199–200
  critical management system
    philosophy for, 204
  customer satisfaction in, 195
  definition of, 189–90, 193, 195–
    201
  employment patterns and, 217–21
  functional "process," 190, 191, 192
  as immediate performance action,
    282, 284, 285
  implementation of, 201, 203–5
  index to difficulty of
    implementing, 16
  new "product," 190, 191, 192
  people and, 202, 206–7
  pitfalls of, 203–5
  plan of action for, 205
  positive and negative aspects of,
    19
  process in, 192, 194, 195, 202
  quality goals in, 197
  radical, 195, 197
  reasons for, 189–93

About the Author

V. Daniel Hunt is the president of Technology Research Corporation, located in Springfield, Virginia. He is an internationally known management consultant, emerging technology analyst, and author in productivity (quality, change management, teamwork), systems engineering (concurrent engineering, and product and process improvement), integrated product development (reengineering and business process redesign), and advanced manufacturing technology (CAD, CAM, CIM).

Mr. Hunt has thirty-one years of management and advanced technology analytical experience as part of the professional staffs of Technology Research Corporation, TRW, Inc., the Johns Hopkins University/Applied Physics Laboratory, and Bendix Corporation.

He has served as consultant on projects for the Electric Power Research Institute, the U.S. Department of Defense, U.S. Drug Enforcement Administration, Advanced Research Project Agency, James Martin and Company, Pacific Gas & Electric, Science Applications International Corporation, Professional Services International, the Pymatuning Group, Maxim Technologies, Arthur Andersen/Andersen Consulting, the Dole Foundation, and many commercial and industrial firms. Mr. Hunt is also the author of *Reengineering—Leveraging the Power of Integrated Product Development, Quality in America, Quality Management for Government, Managing Quality, The Enterprise Integration*

317

Sourcebook, Understanding Robotics, Computer-Integrated Manufacturing Handbook, Robotics Sourcebook, Mechatronics: Japan's Newest Threat, Dictionary of Advanced Manufacturing Technology, Artificial Intelligence and Expert System Sourcebook, Process Mapping, and *Smart Robots.*

A holder of degrees in electronics engineering and management, Mr. Hunt maintains an active schedule as author and international lecturer on business survival, change management, quality improvement, reengineering, process mapping, and productivity improvement, while serving various industrial companies, government agencies, and other institutions as a management consultant.

Technology Research Corporation provides consulting, planning, implementation, and training services to assist organizations in improving their profitability, performance, and survival by applying reengineering and quality management tools and techniques to meet their unique needs.

For additional information, contact:

Technology Research Corporation
5716 Jonathan Mitchell Road
Fairfax Station, VA 22039
Attn.: Mr. V. Daniel Hunt
(703) 250-5136